IN GOD'S CARE*

Other Hazelden Meditation Books and Titles
of Related Interest

The Promise of a New Day:
A Book of Daily Meditations

Each Day a New Beginning:
Daily Meditations for Women

Worthy of Love:
Meditations on Loving Ourselves and Others

Stairway to Serenity:
A Spirituality of Recovery
by Mark L.

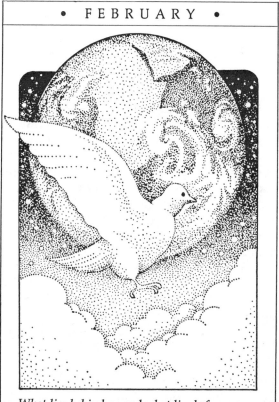

• FEBRUARY •

What lies behind us and what lies before us are tiny matters compared to what lies within us.
—Ralph Waldo Emerson

It is the soul's duty to be loyal to its own desires.

— *Rebecca West*

Our soul's *pure* desires, those that harm no one else, are really invitations from God for us to try new activities, to perhaps move along unfamiliar corridors, or tackle challenges that will carry us closer to our destiny. Fulfilling our desires can expand our knowledge of life, but even more, it can strengthen our trust in our Higher Power.

Perhaps our primary goal is to trust more in our Higher Power's presence, loving guidance, and commitment to our growth. Our Higher Power is our most treasured friend and teacher, our most significant other. We'll never be led astray with the guidance offered us for fulfilling our purest desires.

I will ask God for direction and attune myself to my innermost desires today.

IN GOD'S CARE*

*Daily Meditations
on Spirituality in Recovery*

*As we understand God

Illustrations by
David Spohn

A Hazelden Book
HarperCollins*Publishers*

FIRST HARPERCOLLINS EDITION PUBLISHED IN 1991

Library of Congress Cataloging-in-Publication Data

In God's care : daily meditations on spirituality in
  recovery : as we understand God.—1st
  HarperCollins ed.
    p. cm.
  "A Hazelden book."
  ISBN 0–06–255354–2
  1. Devotional calendars.
  BV4810.I54   1991
291.4'3—dc20   90-55375
                                    CIP

95 96 BANTA 10 9 8 7 6

INTRODUCTION

Those of us in AA and other Twelve Step programs seek to strengthen our understanding of our Higher Power. The Third Step asks us to turn our will and our life over to the care of God, as we understand God. Perhaps we falter from time to time and have to ask ourselves anew what this means.

We can look back to an earlier time in our life and know that a Higher Power must have been protecting us, guiding us, saving us from harm's way. But on a daily basis we often lose our sense of God's presence and feel fearful.

Our security is as certain as our knowledge that our Higher Power is never more than a thought or a prayer away. We may want to feel this at all times, but fortunately our program friends and sponsors remind us that this is a *daily* program of action. "Practicing the presence of God" sums up what we, the authors, believe to be our daily task, and the meditations that follow have been written to help you do that.

Two of us have collaborated on these meditations, and you will hear both of our voices as you read. We each have come to believe in a loving God as our Higher Power after many years of sober Twelve Step living. It's our shared belief that the sustained serenity and joy we desire is guaranteed each time we "remember to remember" that a loving Higher Power is always present, and to feel that presence we must get our ego out of the way. Asking ourselves what God would have us do in a situation, and listening for God's direction, will always clarify what our next move should be. We've taken what we have learned about spirituality from sponsors, meetings, and practicing the Twelve Steps over many years of sobriety and have come to believe that our Higher Power asks only that we cultivate a loving heart and then let it guide our thoughts, feelings, desires, and actions.

We alcoholics and addicts insist on complicating our life. We did it masterfully for years. But the power of this Twelve Step program lies in its simplicity. And simply speaking, our Higher Power is here, now, and in charge of our life. Our assignment is to move our ego aside and follow our loving and sane spirit. We believe we can keep our daily living simple and serene. Let's love and respect one another; let's learn from one another and the circumstances surrounding us; and let's rely on God, as we understand God, to guide us gently through the bumpy terrain.

We hope what we have to share will be helpful to you as you travel your recovery path. Our vision, our understanding of God, may differ from yours, but we share with you the desire for peace and joy. And we have discovered that the more we adhere to the principles of this simple program, letting our Higher Power take charge of our life, the more certain we are of the peace and joy we deserve.

May the days ahead be gentle ones as you cultivate your relationship with God in whose care you have always been.

In fellowship,
The Authors

Solitude is not something you must hope for in the future. Rather, it is a deepening of the present.

—Thomas Merton

Real love is a permanently self-enlarging experience.
— M. Scott Peck

Observing the stately calm of an elderly couple on a park bench or watching children boisterously chasing their playmates; noting the comfort of a worn path through a park or hearing the wildness of wind in a tree filled with chirping birds can bring home to us the miracle of God's world — a world teeming with life, full of contrasts. It's a world that has a special place for each of us.

Letting the rapture of this miracle wash over us changes us wholly, in the wholeness of the moment. We cannot doubt God's love for the universe when we enter undemandingly, unquestioningly the wondrous current of life.

And how remarkable, how miraculous our recovery is: yet another gift from God, one we show gratitude for each time we offer a loving glance or thoughtful, caring remark to another of God's miracles.

We will grow in understanding and appreciation and self-assurance with each loving action we take.

I will help myself grow today.

*Not only then has each man his
individual relation to God, but each man
has his peculiar relation to God.*
— George MacDonald

Each of us sees and experiences God in a way somehow unique to us. No two people see things exactly alike. That's why our program has no dogma. Each of us is encouraged to follow a spiritual path that seems to have been created for us. And we need not worry if we're on the right one, because every path leads to God. Would God let us lose our way? Of course not. We will know if a course correction is needed, and God will lead us to it.

Each of us understands God in a way no one else does. There's a place in God's love for each of us. And out of that place we can bring light to other people, just as our own special people have brought their light to us.

I will cultivate my unique vision of God so that I may bring light to someone else.

You have freedom when you're easy in
your harness.
— *Robert Frost*

Flowing with whatever comes to us in life eases us through each day's demands. When we resist change and the unfamiliar, we imprison ourselves and hide from God's invitations to grow. Only when we willingly experience God's lessons with trust and faith, and see them as blessings, are we able to wholeheartedly join in the stream of life.

With God in our life, what we once regarded as coincidence becomes the order of the day. Every situation and encounter weave threads in the tapestry of our life, as we in turn are threads in the tapestry of others' lives.

The pattern unfolds every day that we live trusting that each moment is meant to bless us, educate us, and invite us to contribute our unique and necessary talents. God is here, now, guiding us. We only need to peacefully follow.

I will take it easy today in the sure knowledge that God will provide me with whatever I need.

Do not be unnaturally humble. The thought of your mind, perchance, is the thought of God. To refuse to follow that may be to disown God.
— Frederick William Robertson

How often has a thought that was strangely appealing entered our mind, but we dismissed it? It might have been an impulse to compliment someone. Or, spotting a glum-looking friend, we may have wanted to ask if we could help. How often have we stifled such thoughts for fear our words might be taken amiss? After all, we remind ourselves, we aren't God.

But we don't have to be God to have Godly thoughts. When we won't believe that we are in tune with our Higher Power, aren't we saying that God can't communicate with us? Aren't we putting a limit on God's power? Whenever we ask for God's help, our mind is at one with God. And whenever we feel out of sync with God, we need only change our mind. We know when we are not thinking Godly thoughts. And we know when we are.

———

My mind can be at one with God. Today I will give my thoughts to God.

*Success is a process, a quality of mind
and way of being.*
— *Alex Noble*

As we think, so we are. And we can use our positive thoughts for successful living by keeping our mind on God's presence in our life, by accepting God's love, and by being willing to trust God's care and direction in our life.

We won't experience failure, doubt our worth, nor question our purpose when we commit our life to the care of God each morning as we prepare for the day. The days will flow more smoothly when God leads us on our journey.

Serenity, joy, and even success can come to us when we let God into our life. Our decisions can be made with confidence when they are directed by God's will.

I will remember God today and find peace and happiness.

I hate to advocate drugs, alcohol, violence or insanity to anyone, but they've always worked for me.
— *Hunter S. Thompson*

In a way, our addictions and the resultant insanity have worked for many of us too. How else would we have found this program and the peace and serenity that have come to us? Our addictions eventually brought us to a better life we had only imagined. We had to walk on a painful road before we could begin our recovery. Then, we had to discover the power of surrender. So it is with other aspects of our life. We have defects — perhaps even some remaining addictions — that still cause us pain.

We'll continue to experience pain as long as there are character defects in our life that we are unwilling to turn over to God. But in that sense they *are* working for us because they nag at us to surrender to a Higher Power.

I will use the pain in my life as a spiritual guide.

*The events in our lives happen in a
sequence in time, but in their significance
to ourselves they find their own order.*
— Eudora Welty

We will experience no coincidence today. All
situations that transpire in the next twenty-four
hours have their purpose. No single event, not
the tired, hurried smile from a boss, the phone
call from a frantic friend, or the cold response
from a co-worker is without impact on our current perception of life. However, we shouldn't
try to evaluate the full significance of any passing
event without God's help. Letting our Higher
Power offer us clarity regarding the circumstances
in our life will ensure a healthy perspective.

We've all experienced trauma because we exaggerated a problem rather than calmly let our
inner wisdom guide us. We're only an impulsive
thought away from a flurry of problems. Likewise, we're only an instant away from peace and
enlightenment. The quiet mind will be ever
present if that's our wish.

*I'll truly understand the events of today if I quietly let
God reveal their significance.*

Love it the way it is.

— *Thaddeus Golas*

It's easy to love people who are like us, who may have been raised the same way, educated the same way, share the same values, or have had many of the same experiences. It's not as easy to love people who seem different. But if we are to fulfill God's plan for us, we should try.

It's not easy, either, to love the way we feel sometimes, or the unpleasant things that happen to us. But, like the people who are "different" from us, even our negative feelings need to be loved. Our fears, frustrations, pain, boredom, despair — these are part of us and they oftentimes have a greater purpose.

We may not think it's possible to love how we feel, but we can make the decision to love everything about ourselves — and then we can see what happens. We may not know God's purpose, but we may understand better if we learn to love ourselves the way we are.

I don't know God's plan for me, but I accept myself and others in love.

*Solitude is not something you must hope
for in the future. Rather, it is a deepening
of the present.*
— *Thomas Merton*

We can take a few moments, *right now,* to
really quiet ourselves, and not think of anything.
We can give our mind an unexpected rest, and let
the peace of God's care envelop us like a soft
blanket.

In these moments of quiet, we discover solitude. We realize that solitude is available to us in
a moment's decision. Within solitude we find
God's promise of serenity, and we're renewed
once again. And we can find this renewal again
and again in the serenity that awaits us each moment we choose solitude.

The pace at which most of us live is so tiring,
and our busyness depletes our physical, emotional, and spiritual energy hour by hour, day by
day. The renewal we long for is ours; we just
need to make the decision.

*I'll be quiet, now, and feel renewed and in touch with
God.*

Relying on God has to begin all over again every day as if nothing had yet been done.

— *C. S. Lewis*

We often try to turn our will and our life over to the care of God, as we understand God, but we're not always successful. We are human: We change our mind. We talk ourselves out of our good resolutions. We forget. We fall back into old, destructive habits of mind and mood.

But all we have to do is *make a decision*. We don't have to do the actual turning over. We are, in fact, incapable of sustaining this action. But we can, very simply, make the decision. Surprisingly, when we do, turning over our will often gets taken care of for us. We find that we are indeed enjoying what seems to be God's will for us. The secret lies in making the decision as often as needed. We can decide daily or even hourly. We can, in fact, rely on God every time we need help.

This day and every day, I will decide to rely on God all over again.

*Whatever you may be sure of, be sure of
this, you are dreadfully like other people.*
— *James Russell Lowell*

Sharing our many experiences with our friends
in Twelve Step meetings helps us understand how
very similar we all are. We are unique only in the
sense that each of us has a special contribution to
make in life, one not quite like anyone else's.

Keeping secrets from others can make us fearful. We think, *Could they really like me if they knew
this?* Yet we feel profound relief when we share
our most shameful secrets in a meeting and the
men and women listening to us don't blink an
eye.

We no longer find rewards from pretending
we're someone we're not. Our greatest reward
now is the peace we experience from not having
anything to hide. We have learned genuine humility and that we are equals with other people.
No better, no worse.

*Today I will enjoy the serenity of having no more
secrets and will celebrate my humanity.*

*People who lean on logic and philosophy
and rational exposition end by starving
the best part of the mind.*

— J. B. Yeats

It's a bitter pill to swallow, but our intelligence only gets in the way when we're dealing with things that really count: our feelings and how we express them.

Love is the be-all and end-all. If we are capable of loving, we have nothing to worry about. If we're having trouble expressing our loving nature, our priority must be to remove the barriers. One of those barriers is our belief in the overriding importance of our intelligence.

Intelligence is like good looks; they are both unearned. And we can be sure that our Creator does not evaluate us on the basis of how intelligent we are. If we ask, God will help us overcome our reliance on our intelligence and all other handicaps that keep us from expressing love.

The best part of my mind links me to others, and to God.

Courage is very important. Like a muscle,
it is strengthened by use.
— *Ruth Gordon*

All of us fear the unfamiliar at times; and it's nothing to be ashamed of to occasionally feel frightened by everyday events. We can still forget that God is always with us and, thus, allow fear to take over.

We're learning in recovery, though, that we can empower ourselves through the magic of belief. Acting as If we feel that extra bit of courage and that we sense God's presence protecting us can dissipate our fears and bring us new confidence. In doing this, we will gradually come to know the inner resources God has given us. The more we acknowledge our courage, the more it becomes a working part of our life.

We often unnecessarily complicate matters by thinking we have to face things by ourselves. We forget that our spiritual program offers us ready relief from the terror of feeling alone. God offers us the strength and courage to meet each challenge. We only have to accept.

I will remember God's presence today and discover the courage to face my fears.

Do not be afraid of the ego. It depends on your mind, and as you made it by believing in it, so you can dispel it by withdrawing belief from it.
— A Course in Miracles

Some of us are fond of saying "the devil made me do it" when we've done something we're not too proud of. We might as well say "the ego made me do it" because the ego is our own personal "devil."

Sometimes we like to claim that we weren't in complete control of our actions, that we were overcome by an irresistible urge. We can't, however, say that with a clear conscience. At one time in our addictive past, maybe, but not now. Now, we can be responsible. An urge can overcome us only to the extent that we let it — only as we give it the power of believing in it.

We have a choice. We can listen to the voice of our ego, or the voice of God. How can we tell the difference? By how we feel. The ego's urgings always leave us with some misgivings. God's guidance assures us.

I choose to listen to the voice of assurance.

*Getting people to like you is merely the
other side of liking them.*
— *Norman Vincent Peale*

What does it mean to like other people? It
means giving respect and attention to their opinions and perspectives on life. It means respecting
their feelings, attitudes, and values without passing judgment or trying to control them. Clearly
and simply, liking others means letting them be
who they are and celebrating their individuality.

Openly expressing fondness for a friend is affirming for both people. Our expressions are gifts
that will multiply for us when we've been honest
and unselfish, free from ulterior motives.

We all want to be liked. And we've heard many
times that to have a friend, one must be a friend.
It's a formula that takes only a simple decision
each time we share with another.

My actions will determine whether I'm liked today.

Let us work as if success depended upon ourselves alone; but with heartfelt conviction that we are doing nothing and God everything.

— *St. Ignatius Loyola*

It's a spiritual paradox that the more successful we feel in this program, the more convinced we are that it is not our doing. Our success depends on our Higher Power. None of us can say, "I did it." As the quality of our life improves, though — as we grow calmer and more self-assured — it is only natural for us to feel we've done something right.

We most assuredly have done something right if we are working the Twelve Steps of this program, for it is a stairway to communion with God, a stairway to serenity. The more time we spend on the Steps, the more time we spend with God. It's that simple. So it is true that we work for our own success, and it is just as true that it comes from God.

My success depends on the effort I make in putting myself in the hands of God.

I will radiate love and good will to others
that I may open a channel for God's love
to come to all.
— *Paramahansa Yogananda*

Our spiritual well-being is hindered whenever
we isolate ourselves, whenever we withhold our
care and attention from the group or a friend.
During these moments, our self-centeredness cuts
off our connection to our Higher Power, causing
peace to elude us and fear to set in.

The converse is also true. Whenever we selflessly express love and genuine concern for others,
we can *know* the presence of God and can be ex-
hilarated by that knowledge.

In this, we have freedom. No one else controls
our thoughts or our decisions to give unconditional love and genuine attention to others.
We are in charge. It is up to us to keep the channel
to our Higher Power always open, always freely
flowing. Our spiritual health is our responsibility
and it's an easy one to handle. The only requirement is that we offer love and goodwill to others.

*I will enhance my spiritual health today by focusing
my love on the women and men on my path so that I
may feel God's presence.*

*The hand of Divine bounty proffereth
unto you the Water of Life. Hasten and
drink your fill. Whoso hath been reborn
in this Day shall never die; whoso
remaineth dead shall never live.*
— *Baha'u'llah*

Just getting clean and sober was rebirth for
many of us. It was as though we had been dead to
this world. In recovery it is amazing to see what
we have been missing. Life takes on a new glow.
We can function normally and maybe even excel.
We feel alive.

But eventually we have to ask, "Is this all there
is?" Our physical recovery from addiction may
have relieved us of pain, but this alone doesn't
bring us happiness. We aren't really reborn unless
our recovery is also spiritual.

As we learn to love, to trust, to feel comfortable
among others, we begin to sense spiritual energy,
and we explore this in the beauty of nature, the
radiance of an act of kindness, the warmth of a
tender touch, the growing faith in a power greater
than ourselves. These can mark our progress as
we are guided in this new life.

I give thanks to God for my rebirth.

Forgiveness is the key to action and freedom.
                              — Hannah Arendt

Resentments keep us in the past, a past that can never be relived. Resentments keep a stranglehold on our mind. They keep us from appreciating the beauty of a moment. They stop us from hearing the loving voices of friends. We forget that we have a mission to fulfill God's Divine plan for our life.

Fortunately, we can shake this hold on us, and our freedom comes when we decide to forgive whatever transgressions are made against us. This decision, with some practice, can become second nature.

Clearly the choice to resent no one is our opportunity to free our mind and heart for the real activities God hopes we'll attend to. Our purpose in this life goes unfulfilled when we're consumed by resentments. Now we have a program of recovery to help us develop a forgiving heart and find the peace and joy that are part of God's will for each of us.

Holding resentments against others hurts me. Forgiveness can make me glad I'm alive today.

*It takes about ten years to get used to
how old you are.*

— *Unknown*

If it is hard to adjust to our age, how much
harder it must be to realize we can't even run our
own life with any degree of competence. Until we
get used to that idea we will keep having living
troubles. Accepting our incompetence doesn't
have to take forever, though. The Third Step is a
shortcut that requires no action, only a decision.

Once the decision is made to turn our will and
our life over to the care of God, things begin to
happen. We are likely to find ourselves being
drawn to spiritual people. Maybe we'll read a
book or hear something as simple as the lyrics of
a song that speak to us in a special way. God is
acting on our decision. And we find ourselves a
great deal happier in God's care than our own.

*I'm getting used to the idea that God does a better job
of running my life than I do.*

*Self-pity in its early stages is as snug as a
feather mattress. Only when it hardens
does it become uncomfortable.*
— *Maya Angelou*

Some days we grasp at self-pity like a blanket
on a cold night, and we are momentarily comforted. However, extended periods of self-pity
will undermine our primary purpose, which is to
be at peace with ourselves and others so that we
may know freedom from our addictions. Thus
our self-pity prevents us from carrying a message
of hope to fellow sufferers, that they too can find
release from their suffering through the Twelve
Steps.

Staying clean and sober are gifts available to
all of us when we cultivate gratitude. We can be
grateful for this program that has brought manageability and serenity to our life, and that leaves
us little room for self-pity, anger, or impatience.
Our mind will be willing and open to receive
God's guidance and support when we let go of
our self-pity.

*Today I will stay free of self-pity so I can receive God's
strength.*

When I came in, they told me, "Let us love you until you can learn to love yourself."

— *Anonymous*

It takes a long time to learn to love ourselves. So many things we've done seem hard to forgive. We might be trying to dig out from under tons of negative garbage, negative images. Fortunately, our friends in this program do love us. That will sustain us as we try to get the picture of ourselves back into proper focus.

The thing we must get locked firmly in our mind is that it's all right to be who we have been and who we are now. We know how to repair the damage now. Our program shows us the way to recovery, the way back to genuine esteem in ourselves as God's creations. God made us, and always loves us just the way we are.

———————————

I will try to love myself, remembering that God and other people love me as I am.

Fearful as reality is, it is less fearful than evasions of reality.
— *Caitlin Thomas*

We've become much less fearful of reality since we've come to know the principles of this program. Just about anything could have made us fearful in past years. No doubt practicing our addictions gave us a false courage for a while. But then we could no longer keep the fears away.

How do we keep fear at bay now that we're free of our addictions? Most of us have begun to rely on our Higher Power for courage, understanding, and acceptance. The challenges that we're offered are opportunities from God for our advantage. When we're in God's care these challenges are manageable, and we need no longer fear them.

We can conquer our fears as we take advantage of the help, guidance, and courage that come from God.

I know that God will be there for me through every challenge today.

*God insists that we ask, not because He
needs to know our situation, but because
we need the spiritual discipline of asking.*
— Catherine Marshall

An omniscient God must know what we desire
before we ask. God knows that what we really
need most is reliance on God. And how do we
develop reliance? Like most other things, by
practicing.

If it weren't for the need to remind ourselves
daily or hourly that all power flows from our
Creator, we could just say a quick prayer at the
beginning of each week, or each year, and be
done with it. Surely God could fill our requests a
year ahead of time. But getting our wishes granted
isn't the purpose of prayer. Getting to know God
is the purpose.

---

*I need to be in touch with my Creator every hour of
the day.*

*If you keep saying things are going to be
bad, you have a good chance of being a
prophet.*
— *Isaac B. Singer*

We all know men and women who are too
often critical and negative. Sometimes we, too,
are these people. And when we fall into this trap
of negativity, our life becomes unnecessarily
complicated.

Any behavior we commit to practicing regularly is strengthened, whether it's positive or
negative. It benefits us then to practice developing and holding a positive outlook rather than a
negative one. Making the decision, each day, to
quiet our mind, clearing it of negative expectations, is not a mysterious or difficult undertak-
ing. It is rather an opportunity to influence in
meaningful ways the many experiences we're
destined to have.

We're empowered by claiming responsibility
for how we perceive and respond to our opportunities, and thus for who we are becoming.

---

*I will look at today as a day full of promise with hope
and gladness in my heart.*

Seize the opportunity by the beard, for it is bald behind.

— *Bulgarian proverb*

Through laziness or inattention, we often miss opportunities to grow. Maybe we don't play our hunches or listen to our intuition. Maybe we see an opportunity, but fail to act because we're not sure it's what we ought to do. An opportunity to fulfill a lifelong dream has appeared, but we don't trust our good fortune. A chance has come to use our talent to help someone, but we don't know how the person will handle it, so we do nothing.

And we rationalize. We decide it's a frivolous impulse, a whim that's not worth our attention. We decide it couldn't be our Inner Guide.

God seldom takes us by the scruff of the neck and pulls us to our next destination. God provides the opportunities; it's up to us to seize them. God talks to us; it's up to us to listen.

Today I'll be on the lookout for God's opportunities.

*There is a need to discover that we are
capable of solitary joy and having
experienced it, know that we have
touched the core of self.*
— *Barbara Lazear Ascher*

To be alone with ourselves, undistracted by a
friend's voice or TV or a good book, is not all that
easy. We discover the joy of *being* and not always
doing, when we make a commitment to go within
and seek the support of our Higher Power.

We are nurtured in times of quiet solitude as,
little by little, we come to know and love ourselves more. We find lasting joy deep within ourselves rather than in outward success, other
people's approval, or mood-altering drugs.

Deciding to leave our distractions for even a
few moments will take courage; we may fear the
unknown, certain that if we really get to know
ourselves, we'll discover we're unlovable. Fear of
the unknown is natural, but it lessens as we ma-
ture in our spiritual life. We are meant to know
and love ourselves as we're known and loved by
God.

*Today I will quietly go within and I will seek the self-
assurance and joy that come from God.*

Love "bears all things" and "endures all things." These words say all there is to be said; nothing can be added to them. For we are in the deepest sense the victims and the instruments of cosmogonic "love."

— Carl Jung

Those of us who've fallen in love can never forget the tender adoration of and the seeming perfection of our beloved, nor the complete abandon we felt. Later, when familiarity cleared our vision, we began trying to control the relationship and, of course, our beloved.

To bind them to our will, we wrap our loved ones in ribbons of care and concern. Or, if we are the least bit insecure, we become restrictive and possessive. Yet, as we experience the love of those who are helping us find our way — in recovery and, through them, to the love of God — we come to understand that love must be free. God's love does not insist on fidelity, good taste, or common sense. Why then should we demand more of those we love?

No person is my private possession, no behavior the price of my love.

The luxury of doing good surpasses every
other personal enjoyment.
— *John Gay*

Helping a friend move, listening to a troubled spouse, or doing a special favor for someone can help us in many ways. And our rewards are often quickly evident. When we help someone else experience a few moments of relief or happiness, our own needs are often addressed in loving and sometimes mysterious ways.

God will always make sure that our own needs are taken care of. Letting our needs be taken care of in God's time means we have more time to think of others.

When we work this program, we grow in our capacity to love others through our acts of kindness. And we begin to love ourselves more. As this love grows, we are changed—profoundly and forever.

God's hope for me is that I grow in my capacity to love.
I can plant many seeds today through acts of kindness.

Take all the pleasures of all spheres
And multiply each through endless years,
One minute of heaven is worth them all.
— Thomas Moore

The pursuit of pleasure long occupied too much of our time and attention. Whether through gratification of our senses or the satisfaction of power and prestige, we wanted more pleasure. And however much we got, it never seemed enough. In fact, in one way or another, chasing pleasure always brought us pain.

It wasn't until this pursuit led us into one of life's dead-end alleys that we discovered it wasn't *pleasure* we really wanted, but *happiness*. We are learning in recovery to put aside our own desires, at least momentarily, and to offer someone a helping hand. In this unselfish instant we find happiness. And we find God. For in helping others, we open a channel to Divine guidance.

Pleasure is an empty, selfish pursuit. I choose the happiness of sharing with my brothers and sisters and finding God's will for me.

To avail yourself of His certain wisdom,
ask of Him whatever questions you have.
But do not entreat Him, for that will
never be necessary.

— *Hugh Prather*

Most prayer is asking for something. Even in prayers of gratitude we are asking God to notice who we are and that it is *we* who are grateful. But God knows who we are, of course, and what we need and want before we have even thought of it. Why pray then?

Because it keeps us in touch with our Maker. It reminds us who we are, children of God, under Divine protection. Sometimes we forget this in our busyness, and our life becomes less than fulfilling.

Asking God for help when we are stumped or confused brings us clarity and assurance. Asking God to provide for us is unnecessary, but reassuring. Asking keeps us in touch with the source of our power. And that makes all the difference.

Today I'll keep the lines of communication between me and God open.

The first duty of love is to listen.
— *Paul Tillich*

To be a better listener is a simple decision to make, but not so easy to carry out. How quickly our mind is distracted from a friend to an interesting looking stranger or to a tantalizing fragment of conversation from across the room. The person asking for our attention is not there by accident. As we attend to the moment, we learn our part in God's plan — our next steps. When we listen closely to what someone is saying, we pay homage to God by the simple act of honoring another person's worth.

Each day is vibrant with opportunities meant to bless our life. And every opportunity is known and available to us when we listen with our ears, our mind, and our heart. We grow in our understanding of God's love every time we quiet our mind to all but the message in each moment.

I can be attentive and quiet while in the presence of God shining through the words of my friends today.

*If we go down into ourselves we find that
we possess exactly what we desire.*
— *Simone Weil*

We were driven by insatiable desires, unable
to get enough of anything — material possessions,
physical sensations, social acceptance. Whatever
massaged our ego, stimulated and sated our ap-
petites, created illusions of grandeur, tickled our
senses, carried us to dreamland, took our mind
off our troubles and made us forget — that was
what we wanted. Yet the fulfillment of these desires left us spiritually bankrupt.

Our recovery begins with the discovery that
we already have what we need, that love is what
really matters. And we get love by giving love.
When we invest our time in doing loving things,
going deep into ourselves to learn God's will for
us, we get even more than we hoped for.

*Today I want to know my Higher Power's will for me
and trust that I have the love I can never give too
much of.*

*Happiness in the older years of life, like
happiness in every year of life, is a matter
of choice—your choice for yourself.*
                              — Harold Azine

We empower ourselves every time we accept
responsibility for choosing the thoughts and feelings we act on. Choosing behavior that encourages happiness is often as easy as any other choice,
and the rewards are certainly greater than when
we act out of fear or resentment. Events we had
expected to be troubling, and relationships where
we had predicted conflict, are more likely to turn
out surprisingly smooth when we come to them
with a happy attitude. We will feel better about
ourselves when we are able to respond to other
people with encouragement and hope.

We complicate our life unnecessarily when we
choose to act out of meanness, self-centeredness,
or self-pity. Actions arising from negative attitudes eventually lower our self-esteem and block
our connection to God. Happiness is often as
simple as making the decision to take charge of
who we are now, as we rely on God's will for us.

*I will choose happiness today as I rely on God's will
for me.*

*It is not true that life is one damn thing
after another — it is one damn thing over
and over.*
— Edna St. Vincent Millay

If there's one thing you can say for addicted people, it's that we're hardheaded. It takes us a long time to be convinced that something is bad for us, particularly if it feels good momentarily. It's also hard to convince us that something is good for us, even when we desperately want to stop feeling bad. As a result, we've spent much of our life doing things over and over — spinning our wheels.

Luckily, there's a cure for this. It's called *turning it over.* We quit trying to figure out what is good or bad for us, or even what is in our best interest. We know that, on our own, there's no sure way we can tell. Instead, we ask a higher authority to handle it for us. That authority is God.

Instead of continually trying to control my life, I'll continually turn it over to the care of God.

Love doesn't grow on the trees like apples in Eden—it's something you have to make.

— Joyce Carey

There probably aren't many of us who feel we're loved enough. The paradox is that *looking* for love is not the way to find it. Abundant love will find us when we make the decision to attentively and unconditionally give it to all the people God has invited to share our life.

Our primary purpose today is to know and give love. Most of us turned to alcohol and other drugs in part because we felt unloved, unworthy, without purpose. This new life we've been graced with—a life filled with opportunities to experience positive ways of thinking, meaningful endeavors, and a family of loving friends—hasn't come to us accidentally or coincidentally. It has been God's will throughout our life that we know love, and be able to openly and freely offer it to others.

God is the caring guide who will help me know love as a result of my willingness to love.

What I spent, I lost; what I possessed is left to others; what I gave away remains with me.

— Anonymous

They say money talks. And so it does. The amount of time we spend trying to acquire money and the things it can buy speaks volumes about our spiritual state. We use money to gauge our success, to measure our community standing, to give us a sense of security. And then we wonder at the emptiness we feel. There may be coins in our pockets, but they can't buy our spiritual needs.

As we look for fulfillment elsewhere, the importance of money recedes. We begin to treasure quiet times with friends and family — and with our Higher Power. We thrive on sharing our experience, strength, and hope with those who have none. We feel rewarded when we brighten someone's moment with a smile. We come to see that we are enriched by what we give, not by what we have.

Today I look for a chance to give to someone in need because this is how I grow spiritually wealthy.

Time is a dressmaker specializing in alterations.
— *Faith Baldwin*

Everything is in a constant state of change. It's easy to see this in the living things around us, which perpetually grow and die, making room for new life. And we are also changing every moment: We form new opinions; expand our knowledge base; discard troublesome behaviors and develop new, more effective ones.

Many of the changes we need to make won't happen automatically. We're fortunate to have the program to guide us in making the changes that will enhance our spiritual growth today.

When we do our Fourth Step inventory, we open the door to making changes in our life. By continuing to work our program through taking daily inventory and maintaining contact with our Higher Power, we come to enjoy change as an opportunity for renewal.

Today I will notice how I'm changing and growing, becoming who I want to be in God.

I was going to buy a copy of The Power of Positive Thinking, *and then I thought: What the hell good would that do?*

— *Ronnie Shakes*

There *is* something to be said for Norman Vincent Peale's outlook on life. Our mind is a powerful instrument, and God has given us the freedom to use it in any way we wish. An optimistic outlook can actually change things for the better. A pessimistic outlook can do just the opposite. The kind of world we see is up to us.

In this program, we are urged to live One Day at a Time. Using this slogan can get us through difficulties. And a positive attitude can bring us even fewer difficulties. Maybe God is trying to tell us something. We soon learn that giving someone else a hand gets our mind off our own woes and helps to banish despair. Before long, we're living on the upbeat without even realizing it — and then positive thinking comes naturally to us.

One Day at a Time, I'll look on the bright side.

*Never forget that God tests His real
friends more severely than the lukewarm
ones.*

— *Kathryn Hulme*

All of us have experienced times when we felt
forsaken, when we were no longer certain that a
Higher Power really existed, was present within
us, and in charge of our life. The unexplainable
death of a friend or parent may have pushed us
to our limit of belief. Or the painful end to a
relationship we'd been sure was part of God's
plan shook our faith.

We can't expect to be free of all strife in our life
just because we walk a spiritual path. By simply
being alive and in relationship with other people
we will know pain as well as happiness.

As we open ourselves to a spiritual life, we
discover a power greater than ourselves that sus-
tains us. This power is available, even when we
suffer beyond our understanding. And we can
rely on this power that fills us with peace every
time we turn over what we can't handle.

Today I will turn over all my concerns to God.

*It is the final proof of God's omnipotence
that he need not exist in order to save us.*
— *Peter De Vries*

Sometimes we get so tangled up in beliefs, concepts, and definitions that we have no choice but to sit back and have a good laugh at ourselves. If we don't at least occasionally find ourselves a little silly, we're in trouble. Our search for enlightenment and fulfillment, noble as it may seem, might actually come down to one thing — self-centeredness.

It's all well and good to seek spiritual truths, but many of us are looking in the wrong places. Do we know someone who could use a helping hand? Is a friend in trouble? Are we doing something to brighten someone's day? Our faith is empty if we put concern for our own soul before the needs of another.

When we overlook what we can do for our fellow travelers, we are missing the whole point. If we are busy being helpful, we don't need to worry about searching for God.

I don't need to look any further than the next person I can help.

In God's economy, nothing is wasted.
Through failure, we learn a lesson in
humility which is probably needed,
painful though it is.

— *Bill W.*

We are so certain at times that we know exactly what we need and how to proceed. But that new job we want or the relationship that looks so inviting may not fit into our Higher Power's plan for us. And at times our struggle to hang on to a person or a particular plan will only lead to frustration and failure.

Often, in retrospect, we are able to see that God had planned greater things for us than we'd imagined. We are humbled when we finally let God take charge. We find relief from the struggle of trying to control our life as the peace of God's presence permeates our mind and body.

Accepting our powerlessness, even though it may at first feel like failure, can result in stretches of serenity we've never before experienced.

I will let go of of my life today and trust in God's plan for me.

*The closed fist locks up heaven, but the
open hand is the key of mercy.*
— *Hindu proverb*

Remembering how we were once driven by
compulsions that would not let us go, we view
our present progress with gratitude. There is not
one of us who can truly say, "I did it myself." We
received help to get where we are today, whether
we deserved it or not. Recalling our past behavior,
most of us no doubt would say we didn't deserve
another chance. Yet, mercifully, we were given a
new start in life.

If we owe this miraculous turnaround to the
mercy of a Higher Power, do we not also owe
mercy to the people around us? How often do
we harden our heart when someone does us
wrong? How often do we hold grudges? Waiting for each of us is someone in need of our
understanding. Each of us knows people about
whom we cherish thoughts of revenge, people
whose behavior begs for our mercy. Do they deserve mercy? Did we?

---

*I can show gratitude to my Higher Power by offering
mercy to others.*

The more difficulties one has to encounter, within and without, the more significant and the higher in inspiration his life will be.

— *Horace Bushnell*

Our Higher Power is always with us, through the joyful *and* the fearful times. We often don't remember to think of God though, except when we're troubled. Then our feelings of terror and hopelessness push us to seek help from God, and with this help comes renewed strength and faith that our life is cared for by a greater power than ourselves.

It seems we shouldn't need difficulties to remind us that we can always rely on God, but it's easy to be complacent when times are good. We can choose to expand and strengthen our relationship with God anytime. Through prayer, meditation, and a conscious attempt to feel God's presence in *all* situations, we'll come to know and trust God more fully.

Today I will not wait for a troubling moment to think of God. I'll feel God's presence now!

There ain't no way to find out why a
snorer can't hear himself snore.
                    — *Mark Twain*

We are sometimes the last to know when we are offending people. Some of our offensive personality traits, in fact, may be unknown to us. That's why it is not always easy to be "entirely ready to have God remove all these defects of character."

Our attitude must be "what we don't know *can* hurt us," if we are hurting others. We become more aware of our shortcomings — both known and unknown — as we grow in the program and hear others speak of their shortcomings. But our success in losing our faults will be in direct proportion to our willingness. God will surely remove our defects, but in relation to our willingness to have them removed.

I'm not always aware of my faults, but I'm willing to learn what they are and ask my Higher Power to remove them.

Today I forgive all those who have ever offended me. I give my love to all thirsty hearts, both to those who love me and to those who do not love me.
— *Paramahansa Yogananda*

In time we come to understand that the forgiving heart is the peaceful heart and we always have the choice to be "right" or to be peaceful.

Forgiveness and love are partners on our path to genuine self-love and self-acceptance, and thus peace. Peace — or serenity — is our goal and is guaranteed to us each moment that we forget ourselves and shine the light of our love on others.

To not forgive, whatever the offense, pulls the shade on God's light. When we harbor ill feelings toward others, we become stuck in the darkness of old ideas, ideas that won't let us experience the growth, peace, and well-being promised us.

When we forgive, we are freed. When we love, we are nurtured. What we bestow on others is returned by God a hundredfold.

Today I will express love through forgiveness and I will feel God's love in return.

*Show me a sane man and I will cure him
for you.*

— *Carl Jung*

We are all a little wacky. When we enter a crowded room and hear someone giggling, maybe we think it's at our expense. If we hear of a friend's illness, perhaps we check our own symptoms. If someone fails to return a phone call, we may think he or she is mad at us. Maybe we lose the thread of a conversation wondering what the other person thinks of us. Perhaps we are a little unbalanced. But who isn't?

In our program, acceptance comes from just being ourselves, warts and all. We have learned that God accepts us and loves us just the way we are.

Today, God is my key to sanity.

*We become that which has influenced us
the most.*

— *Wilfred Peterson*

In the past, many of us ran with a crowd whose main intent was to be high. As a consequence, we generally behaved thoughtlessly, even toward those who were dearest in our life. We weren't surrounded by positive influences and our actions reflected it. We had not chosen a warm, caring relationship with a Higher Power. We felt isolated and suspicious about situations and most people.

Most of us have observed young children who are already mean-spirited, and we can easily guess the circumstances surrounding their lives. None of us escapes being influenced by those forces and factors that, by their daily presence in our life, demand our attention.

Our program for living is daily influencing us to act from a posture of love rather than selfishness. We are thereby growing in our understanding that to give is to receive. We have to continue on our recovery path to ensure our well-being and the well-being of those people who will be influenced by our behavior.

My actions will influence others today, and I want to be remembered as a positive influence.

What lies behind us and what lies before us are tiny matters compared to what lies within us.

— Ralph Waldo Emerson

Behind us are all the things we ever thought and said and did. They're gone, finished, done with. There's no bringing them back.

Before us are our hopes and fears; we don't know how the future will turn out. And there's nothing we can do, for all our yearning.

God is within us. It means that right now, without our trying, without doing anything to earn it, we have been delivered from our past and from our future. In the present we can find the wisdom of the universe. We need only go within.

I thank God for deliverance from my past and future.

Love doesn't just sit there, like a stone; it has to be made, like bread, remade all the time, made new.

— *Ursula K. LeGuin*

Love works through our thoughts, feelings, and actions — it is never static. We are moved as our expressions of love move others. Love soothes, heals, and encourages the fullest expression of who we are meant to be.

God's love is our birthright. We need only open ourselves to this possibility, and we begin to feel the security needed to take the risks each day holds. Just remembering God's love provides strength and ease for today's activities — whether at work or play, we will be less stressful, more joyful.

As we receive God's freely given love, we must give it away and share our courage and strength with others. We pass God's love on each time we share our hope or gratitude or encouragement with a friend. God's love to us and through us will make us whole, will make secure our day.

My love of others won't be idle today.

What the caterpillar calls the end of the world the master calls a butterfly.
— *Richard Bach*

We are often afraid of losing things we value, such as our job, our health, our possessions, or our loved ones. And the more we focus on these fears, the less we are able to cope with life, and the greater the distance between us and our Higher Power. Loss is a form of change that we can grow into. Fear of loss and fear of change go hand in hand, yet when they happen under God's guidance, they can lead to spiritual growth and personal fulfillment.

Although the caterpillar no doubt values his caterpillar self, turning into a butterfly gives him a different view. Each stage in our development entails both loss and growth. And God is always there to offer a helping hand.

Today I will look beyond loss and see — with God's help — what I may become.

*My formula for living is quite simple. I
get up in the morning and I go to bed at
night. In between I occupy myself as best
I can.*

— *Cary Grant*

We need balance in our life. Both quiet times
for introspection and meaningful activities that
take us outside of ourselves enhance our emotional and spiritual well-being.

Too much self-absorption and too little attention to other people can impoverish us emotionally. Likewise, always seeking distractions and
having to constantly be in the thick of things can
cut us off from our deeper spiritual resources.

The least stressful and most productive plan
for our daily recovery is to strive for moderation
in all our activities and simplicity in our self-
analysis. Our inner wisdom will guide us when
we acknowledge the direction from our Higher
Power that emerges in the quiet places of our
mind. Then we can give our attention to other
people and better acknowledge, praise, and love
them.

---

*I will find time for both quiet meditation and involve-
ment with others today.*

He who believes himself to be far advanced in the spiritual life has not even made a good beginning.
— *Jean Pierre Camus*

Just as there are no graduates of our program, there are none who have completed the spiritual course. We are all teachers and students of one another. God frequently speaks to us through other people. To grow, we must be alert to the spiritual messages waiting for us in each person we encounter.

To believe we don't need to grow anymore spiritually is a sure sign that we have more learning to do. It's kind of like boasting about how humble we are. It's one thing to take comfort from our faith; it's another to believe we have arrived.

I will come to the end of my spiritual journey each night, and begin it all over again each morning.

You can't hold a man down without
staying down with him.
— *Booker T. Washington*

It seems that when we're not feeling good about ourselves, we're more prone to gossip about others or criticize even our dearest friends.

Or some days we may think we're in a pretty good place, and suddenly we begin taking someone else's inventory. We then discover that the ground under us has moved; we're no longer in a good place. Criticism breeds personal discontent. Our negative attitude toward ourselves or others multiplies and soon touches everyone we're in contact with.

Fortunately, acts of love also multiply. We can inspire at least two people *right now* through a loving deed or thought—ourselves and the nearest friend. More importantly, any act of genuine kindness is guaranteed to create a ripple of kindness that will finally reach the other side of town, maybe even the far side of the universe.

I will do my part today to spread love to the far reaches of the world.

The biggest problem in prayer is how to
"let go and let God."
— *Glenn Clark*

Too much of the time we try to run things, to manipulate people, to force situations into the mold of our own desires. When we "try" instead of "let," we announce that we want to be in control, that God must take a backseat.

The little word "let" is a big part of our recovery. The expression "Let Go and Let God" is a key to great power. To let something happen is to relinquish control, step back and accept what is. By letting go, we invite our Higher Power to take charge. It's an attitude that summons the wisdom of the universe.

I will Let Go and Let God.

Doing what is right isn't the problem; it's knowing what is right.
— *Lyndon B. Johnson*

Fortunately for all of us sharing a Twelve Step program, we do not have to be worried about always having the right response—to friend or adversary. We still can, and do, act impulsively and forget to rely on our Higher Power's guidance. But every time we take just a moment and quiet the noise in our mind, we'll hear wisdom that will direct us in how to proceed.

We are fortunate people. The Twelve Steps, the wisdom freely offered to us through meetings, and our regular contact with God have made our life more meaningful and spirit-filled than we had ever imagined possible. In every situation we can be certain that we are fulfilling God's will even if our mind is filled with indecision and doubt. How? If our actions encourage compassion and forgiveness, God is guiding us.

Today I will take away any guesswork and act according to God's will.

*Why, then the world's mine oyster, which
I with sword will open.*
— William Shakespeare

We had little doubt, as youngsters, that the world was our oyster, and we were going to make of it what we chose. But somewhere along the line, that oyster got tougher to open. It was our world, all right, but we failed somehow to become a part of it. Many of us felt (still feel at times) that we were on the outside looking in, estranged from our world and its inhabitants.

This feeling changes as we use the tools of our program. We find that being able to help one another with our feelings of estrangement is a gift of our Higher Power. Understanding each other's fears, we can offer comfort. We use the swords of love and friendship to pry the halves of the shell apart — and then the world is indeed our oyster. For we've found, thanks to the fulfillment of the promises of our program, that we have unlimited potential. We are all God's children, all loved, all included.

I want no one to feel like a stranger in my world.

*Happiness may well consist primarily of
an attitude toward time.*
— *Robert Grudin*

What we selectively choose to do and say from the array of thoughts and feelings flowing through us at any given time is defined by our attitude. We are learning now to what degree we can shape our attitude moment by moment. Accepting responsibility for this is a major step in our recovery.

This responsibility can feel like an awesome burden some days. No longer can we blame someone else or a stressful situation for our actions; we are no longer hapless victims of our environment. Our words and actions clearly reflect the attitude we bring to a situation.

We can be thrilled with this responsibility. We can make positive choices about how to express our feelings. Our goal is a consistent attitude of joy and gratitude that will foster blessings wherever we find ourselves.

I will be aware of the thoughts and feelings that shape my words and actions today, and strive to promote joy and gratitude.

*The mind can assert anything, and
pretend it has proved it. My beliefs I test
on my body, on my intuitional
consciousness, and when I get a response
there, then I accept.*

— D. H. Lawrence

We should listen to our body. Sometimes our
body can tell us more about what's right and
wrong than our mind. When an insight comes to
us, or an idea for good, we can feel it at gut level.
And when we are about to do something that
won't work or be well-received, we often feel
instinctively before our mind gets into gear.

Our mind and body, of course, are not separate, so it's not surprising that we can feel things
before we "know" them. Our mind can often be
so cluttered with trivia that only feelings can get
through to us. Intuition is one way God gets in
touch. We need to keep our mental pathway open
to our Inner Guide, but if that channel is blocked,
we can still listen to our body.

Today I attune myself to God — mind and body.

• MARCH •

*As the ripples caused by a flung stone stir the
surface of a whole pond, so your joy-making
shall spread in ever-widening circles.*
                    —God Calling, *March 10*

*"Came to believe": The three most
beautiful words in our language.*
— *Anonymous*

"Came to believe" has become a magical phrase
for many of us. It is indeed beautiful. What did
we come to believe? That a power greater than
ourselves could restore us to sanity. And it has
happened in so many lives that it is a tenet of our
program. The lost have come home; we've been
restored.

As we enjoy the fruits of recovery, though, we
sometimes fail to realize that insanity isn't far
away; it's just around the corner. And when we
experience that insanity, it isn't that God has
moved, but that our faith has wandered and shak-
en hands with the craziness of self-sufficiency.

Coming to believe isn't usually a sudden happening, but a gradual change. And with daily
renewal, it makes our life work.

---

*"Came to believe": those three beautiful words remind
me today that I didn't get here alone.*

*It is the daily strivings that count, not
the momentary heights.*
— God Calling, *January 16*

Progress, not perfection, is the hallmark of our program, and spiritual progress is guaranteed when we stay focused on the simple act of loving ourselves and others moment by moment.

Our longing for the one dramatic spiritual experience that will eliminate all uncertainty in our life and guarantee absolute happiness for all time clouds our vision of the moment. And as long as our sights remain on this hoped-for event, we'll continue to miss the spiritual comfort allotted each step of each day's journey.

We need to reflect daily on the progress we've made. Some of us, immobilized by fear in the past, are no longer anxious. Many of us, lonely and isolated in the past, now have caring friends to turn to. And so many of us are now discovering the relief of sincerely asking our God for help.

We grow spiritually even when we seem to be neglecting our spiritual responsibilities. For this we can thank our Higher Power.

---

*I will open myself with love to each moment today and
know that God is close to me each step I take.*

*Scream at God if that's the only thing
that will get results.*
— Brendan Francis

People who say they know the way to talk to God are speaking only for themselves. How can anyone say with certainty that this is the way, or that is the way? Or what attitude we are to take, or what words to use, or what to ask for, or whether to ask for anything at all? Our relationship with God is a personal, highly individual thing. We have our own assignment on this journey, and each of us comes to God from a different perspective. There is no right way or wrong way to pray.

A simple act of prayer is enough for some of us; just approaching God is restorative. Others are propelled by intense emotion; our need is so great we must shout. *How* we do it, though, is not as important as *that* we do it. The ultimate purpose of prayer is reunion with our Maker. We have gone a long way alone; now we are coming home.

Whether I approach God with a scream or a whisper, I am welcomed.

Love is an act of endless forgiveness, a
tender look which becomes a habit.
— Peter Ustinov

Many of our actions — gestures, the way we walk, our patterns of speech — become habitual. How we perceive and respond to people can also become habitual. Because of painful experiences in our past, we may, for example, still perceive and react to all strangers as threats.

Over the years, many of us have excused much of our harmful behavior as bad habits ("I can't help it that I interrupt all the time."), implying that we don't have a choice and can't change. We are fortunate that in our Twelve Step program, we have the opportunity to learn otherwise.

It may seem impossible to change our perceptions about some of the things that threaten us. This is especially true when our fear is rooted in real emotional or physical assaults in our past. But with God's help, we *can* learn forgiveness.

Each day is filled with small opportunities for us to choose forgiveness. The forgiving heart reaps great rewards.

I am guaranteed God's love and forgiveness. I will ask God's help in letting go of the past and choosing forgiving actions today.

The hardness of God is kinder than the softness of men, and his compulsion is our liberation.
— C. S. Lewis

One reason it's so hard for us to love others as God loves us is that we have no standard in our own experience to go by. The closest thing to a human standard is the ideal love of a parent for a child. God's love exceeds that. The kind of love that God offers us is beyond our comprehension. It is unconditional. We know this because of the innumerable times we have betrayed God, gone back on our own word, and cursed God — only to be welcomed back whenever we're ready, and to find ourselves blessed and comforted.

Someone said, "God has to love us; it's His job." Our program has taught us our "job" is to love others unconditionally too. We don't have to understand God's love; it's impossible. But if we are to find peace, we do have to try our best to imitate it.

Today I will try my best to love others unconditionally, as God does.

*I long to accomplish a great and noble
task, but it is my chief duty to accomplish
small tasks as if they were great and
noble.*

— *Helen Keller*

Today is all we can know about for sure; we
have very limited knowledge of the part other
people or our actions will play in our future. We
can be certain, however, that other people will
affect our personal development, and that our
actions will, in turn, affect theirs.

At every moment we have the opportunity to
be lovingly attentive to the people in our life. We
make a choice at some level to be in their presence and are responsible for the nature and quality of our involvement. We are fulfilling God's
plan for our life when we address every moment
with another person the willingness to express
God's will.

This is what gives our life real importance: to
know that with God's guidance, we can make a
contribution that is necessary and unique.

*I will lovingly undertake the small tasks in my life
today.*

*Every time I've done something that
doesn't feel right, it's ended up not being
right.*

— Mario Cuomo

All of us have had the experience of ignoring warning tugs on the sleeve from our intuition, unhappily discovering too late that we should have paid attention. Or who of us hasn't impulsively followed our intuition and found, to our delight, that what we did was exactly the right thing to do? God speaks to us in various ways. When we need an answer, it often comes to us in unexpected forms: words overheard in a crowded room, a passage in a familiar book. If we are in tune with our Higher Power, the messages we get are likely to be as ordinary as a thought to call someone, or to say "I care" to someone.

We were probably taught from childhood to obey authority, to stifle spontaneous ideas, to disregard our feelings. God has been talking to us all along but we have trained ourselves well not to listen, not to feel. Now we have to learn all over again to recognize our Guiding Voice.

Today I will listen to my intuition. I will yield only to impulses that feel right.

It is a mistake to look too far ahead. Only one link in the chain of destiny can be handled at a time.
— Sir Winston Churchill

How many times today will we think or say, "I wish I knew what was going to happen"? We can find contentment in the knowledge that God will take care of us, regardless of the outcome of any situation. And even more importantly, God already knows the outcome, and we'll know it too when the time is right. We never need to worry; all is well. We're given the knowledge and direction we need when we're ready for it.

If we had known two or three or ten or twenty years ago that we'd be sharing our current journey with non-using, non-drinking men and women, we'd likely have expressed horror and disbelief. And yet we're here, gratefully so, living more peace-filled moments than we would have ever imagined possible. We got here, little by little, with God's care. We'll get where we're supposed to be in the same loving manner.

I will trust each moment of my life to God's loving care.

Love is but the discovery of ourselves in others, and the delight in the recognition.
— *Alexander Smith*

One reason our program has such power to change lives is that it is based on the principle of sharing between people with similar problems and experiences. We are able to help each other when nothing else seems to work because we can identify with one another. We recognize ourselves in each other, making it easier to love one another.

God made us all equal. It is hard for us to believe this until we see others who seem so different, but are really just like us. The knowledge that we are essentially alike — that God gave each of us the same feelings, the same inner needs — comforts us and gives us confidence. That's why it's important that we share ourselves by revealing our feelings.

I will share my feelings with others today and delight in the recognition it brings.

Suffering isn't ennobling, recovery is.
— *Christian N. Barnhard*

Millions of us, worldwide, are sharing this wonderful opportunity to recover. Just knowing we've all suffered intense pain and haunting fears in the past, but that we're now *here*—lending comfort and support to one another—reminds us of the miracle of God reawakened in our life through the Twelve Steps. We know now that suffering isn't a requirement of life; it never was. Suffering was a choice we'd gotten used to making, but one most of us make far less often since finding each other and this program.

In recovery we can realize some dreams that, in years past, seemed impossible. We can become the men and women we'd always hoped to be—and there's no mystery to it. Our assignment is simply to love and serve God, and trust in God, ourselves, and one another. Then, we will know ourselves and become content—we no longer need to question our worthiness or our necessity to God's plan.

I will enjoy the blessings of recovery today. Today will be another adventure that contributes to the realization of my dreams as God wills.

*Whatever a man seeks, honors or exalts
more than God, this is the god of idolatry.*
— Archbishop William B. Ullathorne

We seek many things that have no lasting value. Things such as money, acclaim, prestige, power, fame, popularity, recognition, respect, good looks, stylishness, knowledge, and pride can become our idols if we put any of them before God. We also make idols of whatever we worry about. When we devote more of ourselves to anything other than cultivating our conscious contact with God, we create an inner void. The more idols we pursue, the emptier our life becomes.

If we, however, put God's will before the rest and trust that our needs will be supplied, we often find material possessions, good friends, good health, and good sense coming our way.

Whatever I plan to do today, I will try to seek God's will for me first.

God made the world round so we would
never be able to see too far down the road.
— *Isaak Dinesen*

When our addictive behaviors had control of us, we probably would have laughed if someone told us we would be in a Twelve Step program someday. We spent a lot of our time trying to control and predict the future, and we fought anything that threatened the delusion that we could.

When we were ready, our program was there. We discovered that this is a *daily* program, that by letting God unfold our life twenty-four hours at a time we are released from our obsession to control everything. One of the best gifts of our program is discovering that our Higher Power is in charge of every situation. And as a result, our obsessive need to control no longer controls us.

So now we are free to fully experience *this moment.* We can trust we will benefit somehow because each moment is a gift from God.

Whatever God wants me to know today is sufficient.

*Inspirations never go in for long
engagements; they demand immediate
marriage to action.*
— *Brendan Francis*

God speaks to us in many ways at many times.
If we are spiritually alert, we will know it when it
happens. A stray thought occurs; we overhear a
bit of conversation; a passage in something we
are reading suddenly stands out — and we know
we have connected. A feeling of assurance and
peace comes over us.

The trouble is that we might acknowledge this
contact only briefly, and then it slips away. The
time to act passes. The favor we could have done;
the advice or support we could have offered; the
help we could have given or received — all are
missed opportunities.

When God speaks, we must do more than listen.

Today I will act when inspired.

We are all special cases.

— *Albert Camus*

We spend so much time and energy comparing ourselves to others and far too frequently end up feeling inferior. Perhaps someone at work is more articulate than we are, or an acquaintance always seems more striking and self-assured. And most of us know couples who seem to have the perfect relationship while we continue to struggle in ours or have no significant other.

On occasion we might even feel superior to some people—like the gruff man in line ahead of us at the bank or the rude cashier at the grocery store. But in all cases, the moment we compare and thus create a separation between ourselves and others, we deny the blessing of God's all-encompassing plan for each of us.

We are all one in God. When we realize our connection to one another, we learn our task is to care for each other rather than artificially set ourselves apart.

I will look around me carefully today and notice how I'm connected to others rather than how I'm separate.

You should practice humility first toward man, and only then toward God. He who despises men has no respect for God.
                                        — Paracelsus

It is easier for us to be humble before God than before people. When we have to admit we need help, we are swallowing a dose of humility, but if it's just between us and God, it's not as hard to take.

Being humble with our fellow human beings is different. An act of humility before a visible, breathing, talking witness may be frightening. The witness, after all, could be judgmental.

Are we afraid to be vulnerable? More importantly, can we afford not to be? When we can face fellow sufferers and admit the need for help, recovery begins. Humbling ourselves in this way is our introduction to Divine power: through the compassion our brothers and sisters show for us, we come to know the love of God.

I receive help for all my spiritual needs by being open, first to my brothers and sisters, and then to God.

*As the ripples caused by a flung stone
stir the surface of a whole pond, so your
joy-making shall spread in ever-widening
circles.*

— God Calling, *March 10*

We might all have friends who stir up bubbles
of joy within us. We love being in their presence.
A gloomy day doesn't darken their mood, as it
might ours, and we wonder where their joy
comes from. The answer is simple. Somehow,
they have discovered that they have some choice
as to their mood, and in most situations they decide to experience joy. We can choose the same
for ourselves.

Our feelings, actions, and attitudes are within
our personal realm of control. To pretend that
only people and circumstances are what make us
happy or angry is denying what God has given
each of us: the power to make choices about who
we are every moment.

To feel joy is often a decision no more difficult
than to feel sorrow. Choosing to see our blessings,
even in the wake of turmoil, will bring us joy.
And then we, too, can encourage joy in others.

*My joy can be my decision. I'll make joy my mood of
choice whenever possible today.*

You have to have a talent for having talent.

— *Ruth Gordon*

Each of us brings different gifts along on our journey. We all have a variety of talents. We don't, however, always know how to use them. Some people seem to know how to put their talents to good use. Many of us botch them until we get help from God, who gave them to us.

Each of our talents has a purpose. We weren't given them by accident. We *all* have talents. And, of course, combinations of talents. But we don't live up to our potential without God's direction.

I put my talents in God's hands so that I can live at full capacity.

The most exhausting thing in life . . . is
being insincere.
— Anne Morrow Lindbergh

The time-worn statement "Honesty is the best policy" holds special meaning to those of us in the program. Being honest with ourselves and with others is paramount to our recovery. But it's also important for us to define our honesty.

Should we tell people that we don't like them? Should we confess transgressions from past years if it hurts a loved one today? We each have to decide what honest means in different situations. Not acting or responding in accordance with our inner wisdom is a principal source of guilt and anxiety, particularly if we let that wisdom guide us in one instance and not the next.

We'll know a deeper level of serenity when we decide to be consistently honest and sincere with our companions. A moment's pause to let our Higher Power guide us will help us decide the best response for each situation.

I will seek God's guidance as I learn to be more honest today.

*You must be holy in the way God asks
you to be holy. God does not ask you to be
a Trappist monk or a hermit. He wills
that you sanctify the world and your
everyday life.*
— St. Vincent Pallotti

When we get interested in spirituality, few of
us have any intention of getting carried away
with it. We don't consider ourselves holy. We
want simply to make use of the power we have
learned is available to us for the asking. But once
embarked on this spiritual journey, we find that
something is required of us. The love, the peace,
and the joy that come to us — we have to pass on.

This, however, does not mean we have to completely change our way of living. In fact, those of
us new to living a spiritual life are advised to
make no major moves at all. Maybe sometime in
the future we will be called upon to turn in a
different direction, but for now it is enough that
we "brighten the corner where we are." If we
submit ourselves to God's guidance in our everyday life and see where it takes us, we will be
doing all we need to.

I can live spiritually in the simple acts of daily living.

*Conversion for me was not a Damascus
Road experience. I slowly moved into an
intellectual acceptance of what my
intuition had always known.*
— *Madeleine L'Engle*

Intuition is an inner knowledge too easily discounted in our culture. We may also seldom trust our inner wisdom because we've doubted ourselves for so long.

The things our intuition tells us are not made up by us. Our intuition arises from the deep well of knowledge that comes from God. Through our intuition, God may share with us at a particular moment the best course to take or just what we need to say. And we can be certain we'll not be led astray when we've put aside our will and trust only God's.

God offers us the information and guidance we need when we rest our mind and allow the messages to come from within. Suddenly, as if by magic, we'll know what to do.

I will trust my intuition as another source of God's guidance today.

We are here and it is now. Further than
that all human knowledge is moonshine.
— *H. L. Mencken*

Every single day scientists disprove something that was once an unquestioned fact. Today's fact is tomorrow's fable. Today's cure is tomorrow's malpractice suit. We live in an ever-changing world where nothing stays the same — with one exception.

Throughout the centuries, people have undergone spiritual transformations that were mysteriously alike. Isaiah, Buddha, Socrates, Mohammed, Roger Bacon, Spinoza, Balzac, and Walt Whitman are among those whose transformations we can read about. The descriptions told by countless others of us who have experienced spiritual transformations are also strikingly similar. Across the centuries, God's loving impact on human consciousness has remained steady.

I put my faith in a steadfast God.

A man has no more right to say an
uncivil thing to another man than he has
to knock him down.
    — *Dr. Samuel Johnson*

Disrespect can be as damaging when quietly conveyed as when forcefully shown. We don't have to physically push someone aside to express our contempt or anger. We've probably done it many times by icy glares or being vacant-eyed, as though the person "deserving" of our contempt was invisible.

Hatefulness in any form is never justified. It's life threatening, in fact, because it deadens our spirit and the spirit of the person we direct it at. Not only does the other person feel invalidated and violated, but we are diminished by missing an opportunity to know the love that's our birthright from God.

An act of love is an invitation to come alive. We have the opportunity to celebrate life through loving actions toward others. In so doing we celebrate our own life in God.

Today I will replace my impulses to show contempt or anger with loving actions so that I may know life.

Silence is argument carried on by other means.
— *Ernesto "Che" Guevara*

As a wartime weapon, in certain situations, silence can be employed to throw the enemy off balance. Silence has its uses, too, in domestic warfare. Verbal battles can be waged by sulking and silent scorn. Although the tactic may be effective, it does the user no credit. Silence is better used *before* we get into the argument. As Bill W. says, "Nothing pays off like restraint of tongue and pen."

Silence has another function in relation to our Creator. In the din of day-to-day living, we may find it hard to hear the voice of our Inner Guide. And our work may keep us from staying attuned. That's why it's important for us to schedule snatches of time during the day to be still and remember God.

Today I'll use silence constructively, to be still and listen to my Inner Guide.

To love oneself is the beginning of a life-long romance.

— *Oscar Wilde*

Most of us complicate the decision to love ourselves by seeing our human imperfections as reasons for harsh judgment. Perhaps this became a pattern for us as children. But we don't have to let our feelings then control our decision to love and nurture ourselves now.

The small child within each of us is profoundly in need of unconditional love. Expressing love and nurturing ourselves through affirmations, prayer, and meditation will break the control our earlier thoughts had over us.

It may seem too simple to think that all we need is to *decide* to love ourselves. But that's our task, one we may need to do daily for weeks or months. With faith and perseverance, we will see the results we hope for.

I will love all of me today. Even the not-so-perfect parts.

*I was not successful as a ballplayer, as it
was a game of skill.*
                                        — *Casey Stengel*

Life is a game of skill. Unfortunately, not many
of us come by it naturally, so we compensate in
one way or another. Some of us are quick studies;
we do what others do. Some of us go to college,
some go to the school of hard knocks. And some
of us use chemicals. When asked what finally
taught us about life, we sooner or later have to
say, "None of the above."

When we give up and admit we lack the skill,
that's when we learn. God provides it to anyone
willing to say, "Help! I don't know how to do
this." When we earnestly want to know how to
live life fully, and are willing to give up all our
pre-conceived ideas, God shows us how.

*I don't know anything about this life, so I must rely on
my Higher Power for answers.*

A weed is but an unloved flower.
— *Ella Wheeler Wilcox*

We nurture each other's special beauty by our loving actions. We all need to know we're truly appreciated. We may already believe that our life is purposeful, and we may already appreciate our unique talents. And the contribution we're making at a particular time may be evident to our friends or co-workers. Even so, our fears of not being lovable can still haunt us at times.

These fears are easily put to rest when we help someone else feel special. All it takes is a moment of thoughtfulness, perhaps the simple decision to offer a smile or a loving touch. Offering words of encouragement to friends who are feeling helpless, or simply taking time to listen when they need to talk, will assure them that they matter and that we care. Our Higher Power needs us as emissaries of love in the world.

I will help a friend blossom today, and I will grow as well.

*I do not believe one can settle how much
we ought to give. I am afraid the only safe
rule is to give more than we can spare.*
— *C. S. Lewis*

In this hectic life, demands are constantly made
on us — demands on our time, our attention, our
skills. There are demands on all our resources,
both spiritual and material. How can we meet all
the demands? When we try, aren't we in danger
of spreading ourselves too thin and not being
able to satisfy anybody, including ourselves?

We learn, though, both from God and from
experience, that the secret of happiness is in giving. It is the heart and soul of our spiritual life.
We are always happiest when we are giving — of
ourselves, our possessions, our money, our time,
our attention, our tolerance, our patience, our
appreciation, and our love.

It is hard to give too much. The more we give
of ourselves, the more we give to ourselves.

I will give as much as I can, and a little bit more.

The essence of prayer, even of a mystical experience, is the way we are altered to see everything from its life-filled dimension.

— *Matthew Fox*

Prayer can change us dramatically. It can open our eyes to the intricate beauty in the things and people in our life.

Prayer can help us see the people we pray for—whether friend or adversary—with greater clarity and love. Our gratitude for friends is heightened; our resentment toward adversaries lessens. Barriers mysteriously disappear when we look upon our enemies prayerfully.

The Eleventh Step suggests that prayer may be as simple as asking for knowledge of God's will for us and the power to carry that out. We therefore seek God's presence anywhere we are and in anyone we're with. This is prayer as action, as a commitment to fully invest ourselves in life. When prayer is *how* we live our life, we are able to honor whatever life gives us by responding with acceptance and hope.

Today I will look upon the people and events in my life prayerfully, and be open to the riches I am afforded.

*We are born helpless. As soon as we are
fully conscious we discover loneliness.
We need others physically, emotionally,
intellectually; we need them if we are to
know anything, even ourselves.*
— C. S. Lewis

People today are taught at an early age to be self-sufficient. Independence is considered a strength, and dependence a weakness. As a result, we come to believe that we can make it on our own. And we can, but at what cost? Many of us fill our loneliness with chemical substances. Humans are social creatures; we need each other for physical and emotional support, and for a healthy exchange of ideas.

Even more, we need each other for spiritual development. God loves us equally and often speaks to us through one another. We truly learn about our spiritual nature in the loving acts we exchange.

I am never lonely when showing someone that I care.

*Love the moment and the energy of the
moment will spread beyond all
boundaries.*

— Corita Kent

When we quiet our mind, bypassing our
thoughts about the hour or day before, or our
fear over what may come tomorrow, we can more
easily relish each moment—*this* moment. We too
often succumb to the seduction of worrying about
the past and future, which are beyond our control. Our unwillingness to give up this obsessive
thinking keeps the joy and serenity we long for
out of reach. We forget that the power lies within
us to clear our mind and to fully experience the
peace of the moment.

Quieting our mind requires commitment and
practice. We can circumvent any thought and experience moments of peace—a peace that will
become as seductive as our old obsession to worry.

*I will choose to give up worry today and enjoy many
peace-filled moments instead.*

*I came to this program to save my ass
and found out it was attached to my soul.*
— *Anonymous*

God gets our attention in a lot of different ways. For a great many of us, it was through accident or illness, coming close to death. All of us come to this program frightened for our life or our sanity or both. God has our attention.

And now we are learning about the spiritual aspect of our life, the one we had so long neglected. Now we are partaking of God's love — soul food — and discovering that the spiritual life is fuller and more rewarding than anything we thought possible. Nothing we do to please our body can compare to the joy of unconditional love. When we lend a loving hand to anyone, we realize once again that the pain we suffered was worth it to bring us to this awareness.

Today I will look for ways to help others — and bless my soul!

The hand that gives gathers.

—English proverb

The manner in which one endures what
must be endured is more important than
the thing that must be endured.
— *Dean Acheson*

Nearly every day most of us experience a few small, though troubling, inconveniences. Some days we suffer through a major setback and, on occasion, even a personal tragedy. When we trust that God is in our life, and we look for comfort and guidance every moment of every day, we are prepared for any upset, whether minor or grave.

Practicing the presence of God provides us with a refuge, even in the throes of turmoil. In time, as we make this a daily routine, we'll seldom doubt God's closeness or feel forsaken, even when all about us is dark. The darkness will give way to the light of hope in the mere moment it takes to remember God's presence.

We can endure whatever lesson today offers with confidence and hope and the security of knowing that God is both teacher and protector.

I will go through this day confidently in the presence of my Higher Power.

• APRIL 2 •

God does not comfort us to make us
comfortable but to make us comforters.
— *J. H. Jowett*

We weren't in any kind of condition to comfort others when we were in the grips of our addictions. It's only now, when we have been blessed with comfort for ourselves, that we can turn our attention to others. Now that we can, we discover another spiritual paradox: We find comfort in giving comfort. It is part of the "to-give-is-to-receive" principle.

Perhaps we didn't come by our addictions accidentally. There's a purpose for each of us, and comforting others is part of our purpose. God relies on us to carry the message, as those who went before us brought it to us. That's why we can never be complacent about our progress. The minute we isolate ourselves from others, discomfort sets in — for us and for those who need the comfort of our presence.

My comfort depends on being a comforter.

This instant is the only time there is.
— *Gerald Jampolsky*

How many precious moments of sunshine, birds' song, or friends' laughter we never lay claim to because we're lost in our thoughts about yesterday or tomorrow. God has given us *these* moments we're experiencing right now, and in each one is a gift — intended for each of us.

The smile we get from a loved one or a stranger is precious and worthy of cherishing; but to cherish it, we must notice it. When our mind is not quietly and intently immersed in the present, we fail to garner the strength God is offering us every moment.

Our Higher Power is evident wherever we look, but we must *see*; our Higher Power is evident in every voice, but we must *hear*. Our Higher Power is evident within, but we must be quiet and *know*.

I will quiet my mind so I can see and hear and know that God is present, now.

The hand that gives gathers.
> — *English proverb*

Maybe we grew up believing somehow that to give is to lose. We were taught to believe, or came to the conclusion on our own, that when we give away something, we have to do without it; to give meant to experience loss.

Now, our spiritual friends show us a love that demands nothing in return, and we have a different attitude. We discover that when we give in a spirit of generosity, we lose nothing at all. When we share our love with others, we feel loved. When we share a material possession, we feel rich. The opposite is true, too, of course. When we withhold love, we feel unloved, and when we don't share what we have, we feel the loss of something.

There is a spiritual maxim at work here. We can give of ourselves and have everything, or we can withhold ourselves and experience spiritual poverty.

I give of what I have. It is the way to be truly happy.

*Conscience is the perfect interpreter of
life.*

— *Karl Barth*

In a moment's pause, before we respond to a
person or situation, may come a clear message
indicating how we are to act or what we are to
say. In that quiet moment, our conscience calls to
us. Our willingness to pause, listen, and then act
as our Inner Guide suggests, will ensure that our
relations with others will reflect our true values.

Many of us feel God's presence most through
our conscience. Seldom are we truly in doubt
about the proper response to a friend. And yet,
we may still refuse to pause and listen to God's
message — to remember and affirm our values.
And then we experience guilt and shame.

We complicate our relationships needlessly
when we act before we think. Our agitated ego
takes over, and we lose sight of the sure knowledge that God is the director, we are the actors. A
quiet mind lets us hear the directions.

*I will be quiet, if only for a moment, before sharing my
thoughts today.*

The life of the spirit is centrally and essentially a life of action. Spirituality is something done, not merely something believed or known or experienced.
— *Mary McDermott Shideler*

We often think of a spiritual life as a life of contemplation, of distancing ourselves from the rest of the world. Actually, spirituality is action. We can include spirituality in our day-to-day routines whenever we want. We can transform mundane activities into links to our Creator merely by offering a silent prayer.

As we open an envelope or listen to a sales presentation, we can think of the power and the love we are receiving this moment from God. As we hear the ring of a telephone or have the day's first cup of coffee — any number of ordinary things — we can remember that we are here by the grace of God. When we extend a helping hand, we're saying thanks to God. A smile, a kind word, a hug — all are everyday spiritual acts.

I can take spiritual action in ordinary living.

Conceit is God's gift to little men.
— *Bruce Barton*

It's easy to recognize shortcomings like conceit in others. It's not always so easy to forgive them.

We easily love and accept people who are humble, people who show genuine concern for us and others. We're naturally drawn to them as role models. We learn from them that positive, spiritually motivated behaviors are possible, even desirable.

But those men and women we turn away from because their unappealing behavior offends us, can teach us lessons that are perhaps even more important. Their efforts to get our attention are usually a distorted, confused cry for love and acceptance that even they might not understand. We are given an opportunity to learn tolerance, patience, forgiveness, and finally—with God's help—genuine acceptance. Until we can learn love and acceptance for everyone, we won't be able to fully and freely love and accept even the people we're drawn to—or ourselves.

Today I will make a special effort to give honest and loving attention to those who are difficult for me to love.

We must be willing to forgive without limit even as God forgives; otherwise we cannot be forgiven.

— *Nels F. S. Ferre*

Few of us find it easy to forgive a genuinely felt offense. We may be too protective of our ego. Our grievances are too deeply embedded. So in trying to forgive, we often give offense. As a consequence, the effort to forgive becomes an opportunity for us to act as judge and jury, to see someone's error and, magnanimously, not hold it against him or her. Or to make sure the offender sees how long-suffering and tolerant we are. Or to bargain: if the offender will only do such-and-such, we'll forgive.

In such grudging hands, real forgiveness hardly stands a chance. Better that we ask our Higher Power to do it for us. We can help best by asking God to take over. To truly appreciate the healing force of forgiveness, we must be willing to extend it all the way.

I will ask nothing in exchange for my forgiveness.

*When one's own problems are unsolvable
and all best efforts frustrated, it is
lifesaving to listen to other people's
problems.*

— *Suzanne Massie*

Many years ago a sponsor suggested that I visit a nursing home to see my problems in a broader context. I was angry, not realizing that she was trying to show me that my obsessive focus on my problems was preventing me from seeing the solutions. I had forgotten that the solutions lie within the problems themselves. I was cut off from what God had to teach me through each problem.

Troubling situations can be opportunities to explore new avenues of action. We can help each other see these possibilities when we take a breather from our own concerns and listen to those of a friend. The actions we need to take will arise when a problem is shared rather than fearfully hidden in isolation.

I will open myself to others today, and through them, find that God has solutions to my problems.

*If you're really working the Third Step,
your life is no longer any of your
business.*

— *Anonymous*

Turning our will and our life over to the care
of God, as we understand God, is the single most
difficult thing we would ever be asked to do — if
we were asked to do it. But we are not. We are
asked only to make the decision.

But do we even *want* to turn our will and life
over? Maybe not. After all, we are ultimately
responsible for whatever we do, aren't we? What
if we turned it over and promptly lost our job, or
our savings, or our spouse? Pretty drastic stuff.

But wait a minute. When we make the decision, a seed is planted: What if something entirely different, entirely unexpected and delightful
were to happen?

---

*Today I will continue to make the decision to turn my
life and will over to God, and then see what happens.*

Relax, do not get tense, have no fear. All is for the best.
— God Calling, *January 15*

Relying on our Higher Power to take care of us in every situation does not come easy for most of us. It may help at first to think of it in terms of making a decision. Just as we decide to use seat belts or to exercise before breakfast, we can decide to trust that the Higher Power who has safeguarded us up to now, will continue to do so.

There is a plan for our life, one that promises to be for our good. We know this, intellectually, particularly on the days that flow smoothly. What's harder to believe is that the rough days have their place as well. Even more, the rough days often prove to be the most rewarding.

Look back to a crisis that happened last month or last year. God never forgot us, even when we successfully blocked out our knowledge of God's presence. Our ego often stands in the way of our well-being. Anyone may be God's messenger and God may speak to us in the most commonplace event. God will get through to us when we're open to God's message.

I will remember that God is with me and all is well.

If you're going to take out a long-term
car loan, don't buy a short-term car.
— *Spencer Johnson, Kenneth Blanchard*

We're in recovery for the long haul. We don't expect to return to our old, destructive habits. One day at a time we hope to improve on yesterday until all our todays run out. So it's not a temporary repair job we need, but a brand new vehicle. Putting aside our destructive behavior is only a start. Without the right spiritual fuel to keep us rolling, our recovery may be only short-term.

As we think about what has taken us farthest, what has consistently brought us peace and joy, we can agree on love. Our friends and sponsors love us selflessly; they are interested not in our shortcomings but in our progress. And our Higher Power's unconditional love has forgiven us of everything. In passing this on and seeing it multiply, we experience our happiest moments.

I will ensure my long-term recovery by passing on the selfless love I've received.

*When you pray for anyone you tend to
modify your personal attitude toward
him.*
                        — *Norman Vincent Peale*

We experience a wonderful transformation in
attitude each time we, with God's help, suppress
our ego and ask for God's blessings on someone
we envy, fear, or simply don't like. Any action
we take out of genuine concern for someone else's
well-being will heighten our own — many times
over.

Praying may be troublesome for some of us.
But as we've learned the value of Acting As If in
other instances, we can do so with praying too.
There is no formula for praying. Each attempt to
speak to God is a prayer, one that God hears.
Each loving thought we have toward someone
near or far can be considered a prayer. We can
pray in the midst of a crowd, at supper with
family, laying in bed, or on our knees. With practice, prayer becomes easier. Through prayer, life
becomes easier too.

*I will look at my attitude toward someone I'm having
trouble with and work on changing it today, through
prayer.*

The greatest mystery of life is that
satisfaction is felt not by those who take
and make demands but by those who give
and make sacrifices.
— *Nikolay Berdyayev*

What a different world this would be if we knew that seeking fame and fortune, and striving for gain would only bring us discord and misery. Beginning with childhood, we all receive messages that *getting* is the purpose of living: we must have romantic love, sexual fulfillment, possessions, and prestige to be happy. This is emphasized constantly by various forms of advertising, business, and entertainment.

God has a different message: Help one another. We learn from experience in our program that happiness comes from giving — whether it be time, talent, money, or other things. Experience tells us that giving what we have to help someone else makes us a lot happier than keeping it to ourselves.

Today I will put my emphasis on giving.

Life is God's novel. Let him write it.
— *Isaac Bashevis Singer*

So many times we've had all our hopes pinned to the success of a specific plan for the day or a particular outcome to some episode in our daily drama. Too often we were certain that if we didn't get our way, we'd be devastated. And just as often, God had other plans — for which we can now feel gratitude.

Most of us wouldn't be here if we had authored the novel of our life. We would have gone too far in our pursuit of drugs, excitement, the "good life." There's little doubt we would have gone beyond our limits. Fortunately, God intervened, getting our life stories back on course while there were chapters yet to live.

Letting God be in charge of these remaining chapters as they unfold takes away our fear about what's coming. We know God's plan for us will take us where we need to go. We know that our purpose is still being fulfilled — or we wouldn't be here. We know that God's care will keep us safe. Our care for God and one another will keep us serene.

I'll rest today and let God be in charge.

*God is no enemy to you. He asks no more
than that He hear you call Him "Friend."*
— A Course in Miracles

It is natural for us to take a bit of pride in
where we find ourselves today. It is natural for
self-centered people like us to think we owe it all
to our own efforts. So it's an imposition to be
asked to turn our will over to our Creator. We
sometimes feel resentful at the suggestion that
God can do a better job of running our life.

We don't even want to think about the sacrifices we might have to make with God in charge.
But God doesn't ask for sacrifice. God is not our
enemy; we are. God only asks, as our friend, to be
included in our decisions.

*My prayer today: Thanks, Friend, for my continuing
recovery. Join me in everything that I do today.*

Example is not the main thing in
influencing others. It is the only thing.
                        — Albert Schweitzer

Throughout our life we've been influenced by other people's behavior and opinions. Many of us were influenced by very poor examples in earlier years. And we may have to pray for help rather than continuing to follow those poor examples now. But all around us are people who are healthy, loving, and honest. We are invited to emulate their behavior.

Acting As If can help us develop new behaviors. We may not feel very comfortable reaching out to a program newcomer or making conversation with someone we've just met , but we *can* do it. And in time, with practice, we'll discover we've added a positive dimension to our character, one that influences the lives of other people who struggle just like us. All of us, Acting As If in positive ways, offer wonderful examples of behavior change. We reinforce our own changes, and each other's, every time we are thoughtful before we act.

With my Higher Power's help, I will be a good example for someone today.

APRIL 18

*How can anybody read the Gospels and
fail to see how Jesus, in his contacts with
all sorts and conditions of people, even
the apparent good-for-nothings and
worse, always seemed to find in them
possibilities for sublime development?*
— *Carroll E. Simcox*

Many of us feel we don't deserve God's love.
We judge ourselves harshly and attribute the same
judgment to God as the strict parent, the demanding teacher, or the punishing judge. We cannot
believe that anyone could accept us as we are,
and so we don't turn toward God.

Why do we feel this way? Perhaps because it's
hard to feel that God could love us when we so
rarely received love without strings attached from
others. Many of us remain skeptical even when
newfound spiritual friends shower us with love.
Though we may not realize it at the time, these
friends are providing a human framework into
which the unconditional love of God can fit. If
these friends can accept us as we are, we think,
maybe God will too. And of course God does.

*When my hand reaches out to another, God's hand
reaches back.*

*To think you are separate from God is to
remain separate from your own being.*
— *D. M. Street*

God has taken up residence within us as our
guide and in the world as our companion. Everywhere we cast our gaze, we will see other homes
of God. We are never really separated from God
even though we often feel disconnected.

As children, many of us dreamed of God as
separate and very far away in heaven. To accept
the knowledge that God is everywhere and is
within us is perhaps strange at first. But as our
acceptance grows through working our program,
we are comforted by the knowledge that we travel
no path alone.

We can harbor no thoughts or desires or prayers
in secret. Our constant companion knows us fully,
hears our every need, cares for us deeply, and
will ensure our safety every step of the way. We
only need to remember to extend our hand to
God for surefootedness.

*Let me remember God is my guide and constant
companion.*

*It is not up to you to change your
brother, but merely to accept him as he is.*
— A Course in Miracles

We all feel qualified to correct another. We
may not do this aloud, but we oftentimes do a
great job of it under our breath or in our mind.
We are fortunate if we learn that correcting others is not our job. It is seldom helpful to them or
to us. Correction is best left to God, who knows
all the circumstances.

If we truly need to avoid a certain person, God
will direct us. If not, then it's spiritually good for
us to accept that person's defects — perceived or
real — in all their glory. If we insist on seeing
error or guilt, we'll be in the wrong frame of
mind to accept what a blessing he or she is to us.

Every offensive thing someone does is a call
for help. If we answer it with help, instead of
condemnation or correction, both of us are blessed.

I would rather be blessed than be right.

Hindsight is an exact science.
— *Guy Bellamy*

Sometimes we may think life would be much easier if we knew just what to expect when we're trying something new or making important plans. It's true we wouldn't have to deal with the uncertainty of life, but neither would we have the thrill of anticipation that comes with change.

How our life evolves over time, we entrust to God. God is here today, meeting our needs in ways we can't predict. Our role is simply to trust and listen to our Higher Power and choose our actions accordingly. We no longer have to choose the thoughts and behaviors that foster anxiety.

When we quiet our inner dialogue, we're open to what God wills for us and are available for the experiences that provide for our growth. We'll find ourselves relying less on hindsight and more on our intuitive grasp of the moment. We'll know the best way to proceed in every circumstance if we look to God for direction.

Today I will depend less on hindsight and trying to predict the future, and more on pausing to listen to my Higher Power.

Those who cannot change their minds
cannot change anything.
— *George Bernard Shaw*

One thing we all have going for us is the ability to change our mind. Thank God. If we were still stuck with our childhood beliefs, where would we be now? Many of us have gotten into deep trouble — physically and emotionally — by following beliefs that proved wrong. For instance, the treacherous belief that we are self-sufficient, that to depend on others is a sign of weakness. How many of us crashed and burned while holding high the banner of independence?

Disastrous circumstances have forced us to change our mind. Now we know that we cannot get along without others, nor without a Higher Power to guide us. We are still tempted daily to go it alone — old habits die hard — but we can change our mind as often as needed.

With God's help, I can exercise the greatest force for change in my life — I can change my mind.

An ounce of action is worth a ton of theory.

— *Friedrich Engels*

Overplanning, overthinking, and too much talking often hinder the actions that can bring real growth. We know this, and yet we still get trapped, usually by our fears that we'll not proceed perfectly.

Life is the process of making progress. We learn by doing, not just by thinking. We can make our forward steps more easily when we ask God to share the journey, but *we* have to put one foot in front of the other. And that usually leads us to someone else in need.

How many times have we felt stuck or depressed or obsessively fearful, only to discover our head clearing and our heart calming when we got out of the house, out of ourselves, and focused on someone else?

Helpful actions energize us and give us hope. They connect us to our Higher Power and make all the difference in our daily spiritual progress.

I will not sit and obsess today. I'll go out and find someone in need.

God creates out of nothing. Therefore until a man is nothing, God can make nothing out of him.

— *Martin Luther*

To bring our addictions under control, we had to surrender them — and our willpower — to a higher authority. God relieves us of our compulsions as soon as we admit that we are powerless over them. But surrender doesn't end there. If we wish to move beyond that point — to grow spiritually, to gain peace of mind — relinquishing our self-will must become habitual. We must give God a clean slate every hour, every day.

When we think we have everything under control, we are in trouble. *A Course In Miracles* tells us, "Whenever you think you know, peace will depart from you, because you have abandoned the Teacher of peace." Moreover, it is when we admit we do not know how to run our life that peace returns. We invite God back by turning a deaf ear to our selfish ego.

I offer God a clean slate on which to write my life.

*When we spiritually awaken, our whole
life changes from being hard and painful
to becoming easier and happier, more
pleasant and pain-free.*
— Jerry Hirshfield

Most of us awaken spiritually very slowly.
Looking back on our more dangerous times and
our miraculous survival helps us to believe that
at least something like a guardian angel must
have never been far away. And yet, much of the
time many of us still struggle with the day-to-day
turmoil of our recovery, trying to manage outcomes that are not ours to manage.

We complicate most events by our need to
control what is clearly up to God to control. When
we let go the outcome is generally to our satisfaction. Always, in time, we see that the outcome
benefits us generously. We can't do what belongs
to God to do. Our job is simply to move aside.

The pain of forcing open a door or pushing
through a decision can be relinquished forever if
we simply trust God.

Life is often only as hard and painful as we in
our self-centeredness make it.

I will not try to do God's work today.

*Self-love is not opposed to the love of
other people. You cannot really love
yourself and do yourself a favor without
doing other people a favor, and vice versa.*
— *Dr. Karl Menninger*

Self-love is not the same thing as egotism. As
recovering people, we hated ourselves for so long
that we were crippled by it. Learning to love
ourselves again becomes a form of therapy —
and appreciation for God's creation. And the
delightful thing we learn is that we don't love
ourselves without loving others, and we can't love
others without loving ourselves. How wonderful!

We can't begin to love ourselves, however,
without other people. People are essential, and so
is God, from whom all love flows. We are thankful for God's love and ask God to teach us how to
love others. And the more we practice doing loving acts for others, the more love we feel for
ourselves.

I will practice loving myself today by loving others.

The presence of faith is no guarantee of deliverance from times of distress and vicissitude but there can be a certainty that nothing will be encountered that is overwhelming.
— William Barr Oglesby Jr.

We've all experienced times so seriously troubling that we feared for our sanity: the loss of a job, divorce, or the death of a loved one. And in each instance we learned that the more we relied on our Higher Power's support, the less we stumbled and the more we could allow ourselves our grief and get on with our life, perhaps even stronger and wiser than before.

Facing our addictions and working our program won't guarantee that our future will be free of struggles. Everyone has to live through difficult times, some of us more than others it seems. But we needn't sacrifice our serenity and security through these times as long as we let God share them with us. It's such a relief knowing that nothing has to overwhelm us as long as we remember to let God shoulder the burden we're carrying.

Whatever happens today will trouble me less if I let God handle it.

That was another mystery: it sometimes
seemed to him that venial sins —
impatience, an unimportant lie, pride, a
neglected opportunity — cut you off from
grace more completely than the worst
sins of all.
— Graham Greene

Our old negative ways of handling things —
brooding, complaining, ignoring people — not
only harm us, but they harm others as well. Even
more, they cut us off from God. And because the
small wrongdoings often lead to bigger transgressions, perhaps that's why they take on greater
importance.

Fortunately, practicing the Tenth Step can bring
us back to our senses. Taking an end-of-the-day
inventory can stop a negative attitude that might
have consumed us for days. And when we again
make conscious contact with God, it is as if we
had never taken our little detour. God's love never
strays.

When I am down, I need to take an inventory of my
attitude.

*Character consists of what you do on the
third and fourth try.*
— *James A. Michener*

The need to be an expert right away continues to cause many of us unnecessary pain. When we fail to do something perfectly on our first attempt, we often feel defeated and our self-esteem takes a dive.

Working a Twelve Step program has taught us to expect spiritual progress, not perfection. With patient attention and perseverance we will reach the level of attainment we're meant to reach in whatever we try.

Lasting self-esteem comes when we remember to measure our worth by God's unconditional love. We no longer have to prove anything to anyone. Each new day we seek God's will for us; we accept our shortcomings; and we promptly admit when we're wrong. We are thus free to enjoy our particular abilities and achievements as gifts from God.

I will measure my accomplishments today by how much I enjoy making my best effort at whatever I do. The rest, I'll turn over to God.

Man must cease attributing his problems to his environment, and learn again to exercise his will — his personal responsibility in the realm of faith and morals.

— *Albert Schweitzer*

There's a tendency to blame people, places, and things for our problems. After all, no one as smart as us could get into so much trouble without outside help.

We have to quit assessing blame and take responsibility for our own actions. Most of the trouble we get into is the result of ignoring the guidance of our Higher Power. Others may be ignoring their own inner guidance, but that's their concern, not ours.

Because all people are equal in God's eyes, when we blame others for our problems, we are really hurting ourselves. Looking for someone to blame for a problem only prolongs the solution and puts distance between us and God. Blame is a hindrance to our spiritual progress.

When things seem to be going wrong, I have no one to blame. I will make conscious contact with God and, there, learn what to do.

A loving world will be ours when we extend only love. That means the world does not have to change. . . . The only thing that has to change is our attitude.

—Gerald Jampolsky

*Loving can cost a lot, not loving always
costs more.*
— *Merle Shain*

We are invited to choose and express loving thoughts throughout every day. This often means surrendering our opinions or desires for the moment. It means, quite frequently, honoring another's needs above our own. In this way it costs us. And yet, giving up the struggle for the winning opinion or relinquishing our desire to control plans brings rewards. We will feel peaceful with surrender. We will know that God has entered our consciousness.

If we never surrender, if we never give in to love, we are kept distant from our true selves and the people we yearn to be close to. Our loneliness in the midst of our friends will bring much more pain than the momentary pinch of surrender — a pinch that in reality promises peace.

I will choose surrender over control, love over self-satisfaction with my friends today.

*It's not what we don't know that hurts,
it's what we know that ain't so.*
— *Will Rogers*

Much of our spiritual progress is an unlearning process. So many "truths" we thought we could bank on have turned out to be bankrupt. Too many time-honored sentiments that are accepted as noble truths are misleading, false, or exaggerated.

For instance, contrary to what many of us were taught, God's love isn't dependent on anything we do or don't do. Our happiness isn't found in another person, a possession, or the other places we might look — we need to look inside. We really only gain when we give. Struggle brings defeat; surrender brings victory.

I can unlearn my errors by putting God's truth to work.

*One comes, finally, to believe whatever
one repeats to one's self, whether the
statement is true or false.*
— *Napoleon Hill*

Our inner dialogue can have awesome power.
It often determines the behavior that defines who
we are. We do, of course, have some choice as to
the direction this inner dialogue will take. It's as
easy to affirm our self-worth with positive messages as it is to tear ourselves down with negative
ones. And yet, many of us fall so easily into negative patterns of thought.

As with so many aspects of our life, we become proficient at what we regularly practice.
The regular, preferably daily use of positive
affirmations can make such a profound contribution to our well-being and willingness to grow
and learn, that it can change the course of our life.
All we have to do is develop the discipline to
make these positive messages habitual. In so doing, we bring our vision of ourselves in line with
God's, who accepts us completely as we are.

*The messages I give myself today will remind me that I
am a capable and lovable child of God.*

Just because your voice reaches halfway around the world doesn't mean you are wiser than when it reached only to the end of the bar.
— *Edward R. Murrow*

Sometimes we believe anything from an earlier generation is outdated. With technology, this may be true. But people are not necessarily wiser today. Some time-tested wisdom is sliced to slivers on the cutting edge of what's new. Old-fashioned honor and morality too often are made to seem hopelessly archaic.

The widespread attraction of mind-altering chemicals, the restlessness of many people, the search for a simple, fast spiritual fix — all testify to a hunger that many newfound beliefs have failed to satisfy. We are fortunate to have found in our program an answer to the malaise that afflicts so many people. In its simplest form, it's called love; in its purest form, God.

I thank God that the wisdom of the ages is still relevant today.

Boast is always a cry of despair except in
the young when it is a cry of hope.
— *Bernhard Berenson*

We're easily put off by people who brag about their accomplishments, especially if we're having trouble meeting our own goals. It's more difficult to see the struggling spirit behind the boasting when we're so focused on our own progress in life. It helps to remember that God's goal for us in any encounter with another person is really very simple: that we love one another, wholly and sincerely.

Those whose behavior makes them the most difficult to love, need our love the most. Their lack of inner peace and self-doubt pushes them to the behavior that makes us want to turn away. We need not turn away. God invites us to love all our fellow travelers fully and unconditionally. Negative attitudes and behavior can provide our personal lessons in acceptance and serenity, and we will develop gratitude for these lessons, in time.

I will set aside my judgments today and be open to God's lessons.

Belief consists in accepting the
affirmations of the soul; unbelief in
denying them.
— *Ralph Waldo Emerson*

God seems distant at times. We are all, at times, beset by doubts. Sometimes we think faith is foolish. It's only natural; it shows we still have a healthy ego that is all too eager to run the show. This is nothing to worry about; most of the world's spiritual giants have had dark nights of unbelief.

If nothing else, in life's darkest moments, we can believe in belief. There is an affirmation in each of us that tells us we are in touch with a power greater than ourselves. There are few of us who don't, at some time, believe we get help from a Higher Power. An inner voice, ever so quiet, gently guides us, assuring us we are not alone.

And a little faith is all we need. The Bible says that the smallest amount, no more than a mustard seed, is sufficient. All we need is enough to start with; God takes it from there.

Today I will have faith in my own faith. It is enough

We see things not as they are, but as we are.

— *H. M. Tomlinson*

Many days we wake up filled with confidence, enthusiasm, and gratitude for the blessings that have come to us through our recovery. We are even able to see that some of our earlier troubling moments were really blessings in disguise.

Our more positive attitude today changes our understanding of earlier experiences. And that's the key to how the future will look. If we rely on God's help, we'll come to understand all our experiences as opportunities for growth and fulfillment. We can trust them, live through them, and be grateful for their contribution to our spiritual development.

The attitude we harbor is powerful. We can develop a peaceful attitude and keep it for all time if we so desire. God is always available to help us accept the circumstances of our life.

With God's help I will believe my circumstances are as they should be today.

*Love of certainty is a demand for
guarantees in advance of action.*
— *John Dewey*

Sometimes we seem awfully reluctant to make
the leap of faith. At one time, uncertainty didn't
bother us too much. We trusted our addictions to
see us through any trouble we might encounter.
What, then, is so hard about trusting God?

Guarantees in advance are hard to come by.
One thing we can depend on, though, is the feeling of safekeeping that will enter our heart when
we turn our will over to our Higher Power. Turning it over is an action that never fails to reward
us. Each time we decide that we can no longer
run our life, each time we ask God to do it, things
begin smoothing out. We never know exactly what
will happen when we do this and are often surprised by the turn of events, but we are seldom
disappointed. Even when we are, it's only temporary; the future proves we placed our faith in
the right place.

*I ask for no guarantees today. I will make the
leap of faith.*

*When one's own problems are unsolvable
. . . it is life-saving to listen to other
people's problems.*
— *Suzanne Mossie*

There are times when we get so engulfed in a
problem—whether it's a conflict in a relationship
or a job issue that demands all our time—that we
lose perspective and miss an obvious solution
that may be clear to someone else. Fortunately,
our fellowship encourages us to share our innermost concerns with each other, and we usually
find caring listeners when we do. This exchange
rewards us with the clarity we need. We discover
a power greater than ourselves, a wisdom in the
group that transcends that of any individual.

It's not by chance that we've been invited into
one another's lives—as both teachers and students. What we share in any one moment may
help others better understand their situation, and
their response can enlighten us. Our tasks are to
be honest, receptive, and willing to share and
listen.

*I will seek help for a troubling situation today by
turning to others.*

I never know how much of what I say is true.

— Bette Midler

We often speak with great conviction while harboring the thought that we don't really know what we're talking about. When it comes right down to it, on life-and-death matters, we get most of our ideas from somebody we respect, or from what reason or a strong hunch tells us. There is no ultimate authority on this earth. We have to go on evidence, gut feeling, and intuition.

Evidence is what we see with our own eyes, such as the dramatic personality changes that come over people when they follow our spiritual program. Gut feelings are just that; we know when something we read or hear feels right to us. And intuition is sometimes having insight about something or someone that goes beyond our current knowledge.

Although we don't always know if the evidence before us, our gut feelings, or our intuition is always accurate, we can trust our Higher Power to show us the truth through them.

I will ask God to help me when I'm doubting myself or feel confused.

*We find that as we become more centered
within the Higher Power part of us, our
ego becomes less real, less threatening,
less compelling.*
— Jerry Hirshfield

It's a struggle at times for us to remember that
our Higher Power never moves away. God is as
close as our breath, awaiting our invitation to
take charge. Frequently this strikes us as *new* information. But each time a friend or a particular
reading triggers our recall, we relax, because we
know that God is taking over. Once again we
trust that all is well.

It's our ego that fights giving up control during
the early stages of many of our troubling experiences. We are frustrated again and again as we
try to force what we think is the best solution;
again and again, in the end, after we've finally
given up the struggle, God smooths the path.

This program guarantees us a smooth trip every step of the way. All we have to do is give up
control to God who is always waiting for us to
turn our attention from our problems to God's
presence.

*I will feel peace and joy throughout today because I'll
remember my Higher Power's presence.*

*The chains of habit are too weak to be felt
until they are too strong to be broken.*
— *Samuel Johnson*

The Twelve Steps won't work for anyone unless they are practiced. That's why so many veterans of this program work the Steps over and over. It's a good habit, and good habits — just like bad ones — strengthen with use and time.

Prayer is an important part of this program that becomes as regular as habit, and it's a habit worth getting into. Communing with God at a similar time, or times, every day brings us power for daily living and provides us with a spiritual reserve. Daily contact with our Higher Power gives us special insights into our own actions and helps us look with love on those around us.

Today I will strive to make prayer a habit.

Attachment is the great fabricator of illusions; reality can be attained only by someone who is detached.
— Simone Weil

It is often with some difficulty that we come to understand our need for personal boundaries. We also have to struggle to maintain them once they're defined. Our boundaries are blurred when our desire to be loved and needed by others seduces us into becoming overly involved in their lives. Or when we find ourselves overly committed with tasks and social engagements—even ones we enjoy. We must remember we need time alone, time for the stillness within to nurture us.

Until we detach from the person or the situation that is drawing us in, we can have no objectivity. We also lose our sense of God's role in our life when our boundaries are blurred. God gives us our direction, our definition, our vision, and our understanding whenever we ask.

I will take time with my Higher Power today to remember my boundaries.

*Often we attack and make ourselves
enemies, to conceal that we are
vulnerable.*

— *Friedrich Nietzsche*

Our mind is a wondrous but perverse instrument. Wondrous because it puts us in touch with every aspect of our reality. Perverse because it is easily turned against us. Unwittingly, we attack ourselves when we attack another. As we lash out, too often it is our own mirror-image we are attacking.

Fortunately, we can use our mind to change our mind. Instead of attacking another, we can say to ourselves, "This is my brother. This is my sister. We are spiritually joined. We share the same set of feelings, the same wants, the same need for love. What I see in them I see in myself. Do we, God's children, deserve condemnation?" The answer, of course, is no.

I will remind myself today that attacking another is self-destructive. With God's help, I can see the other person as myself.

Man needs difficulties; they are necessary
for health.

— *Carl Jung*

Sometimes we think a life free of all turmoil would bring us total happiness. And yet experience teaches us that our burdens and conflicts push us to think creatively and to utilize the tools of our program. In the process of turning to others and to our Higher Power for clarity and direction, we grow. Our progress is timely. All of our experiences—the tough ones along with the joyful ones—provide the lessons we need to prepare us for the opportunities that will arise in the future.

Our Higher Power doesn't intend for us to experience pain. We are given freedom by God to choose, and we often choose a path where our attention is focused on ourselves rather than on our Higher Power. Our pain and suffering arises as we learn the futility of self-will. We can then turn within for the wisdom that immediately frees us from unnecessary pain, and reclaim the serenity that is ours every time we acknowledge God as our companion.

I will look upon today's difficulties as reminders to turn to God for serenity.

*He prays best who does not know that he
is praying.*
                              — *St. Anthony of Padua*

Prayer at its best is an attitude, an awareness
of God's presence. It's a feeling that we are not
alone, no matter where we are or what we're
doing. It is a thankfulness, a silent appreciation of
and communion with our source.

Most of all, prayer is stepping back and letting
go. It is a conscious awareness that we are the
instruments of God's will, that our greatest fulfillment and satisfaction come in letting that will
— not ours — prevail. The best prayer is remembering that our self-will consistently gets us into
trouble and that listening for God's will is the
way out.

*My prayer today is to give up my self-will and re-
member God.*

*A loving world will be ours when we
extend only love. That means the world
does not have to change. . . . The only
thing that has to change is our attitude.*
— *Gerald Jampolsky*

We are powerless over so much: the weather, a
tulip's sprouting, the multitude of people and
events claiming our attention. We often wear
ourselves out trying to control the uncontrollable.
We could, instead, be at peace.

A tiny change in perspective promises huge
and positive ramifications. We need only to quiet
our mind of the clutter of frustrations that inspire
our myriad strategies of control. Then, in their
place, we can focus our energies on this decision:
to respond to everyone we can with love.

For many of us, simply to believe in the unconditional love of God is the decision we need to
exercise daily. As our belief in God's love for us is
strengthened, we find it easier to pass this love
on to other people.

Each time we show unconditional love to
someone in our life, our awareness of the love
available for us grows. In this is our true power.

*The more love I express today, the more of God's love
I'll feel.*

*True denial is a powerful protective
device.*

— A Course in Miracles

Denial has gotten a bad reputation in recovery circles. One of the greatest obstacles to recovery from addiction is denial. Who would seek help for an illness that doesn't exist? Many of us resisted help, suffered needlessly, and caused others to suffer while we went on denying that anything was wrong.

But sometimes denial can be a good thing, especially when it comes to fear. When we are afraid of anything, we are saying it has the power to hurt us. We give fear power by believing in it. But if God is for us, who can truly hurt us? Our fears are of our own making. When we deny the ability of any ungodly thought to bring us down, we are using denial properly.

My fears can hurt me only with my permission.

One must never, for whatever reason,
turn his back on life.
 — *Eleanor Roosevelt*

We are not here without purpose. We are being called to fulfill a destiny. When we look around, we'll see men and women who have been invited to share this spirit-filled journey. As sharing, caring members of the recovering community, God is orchestrating our life and our growth as individuals.

Our program has given us the gift of rebirth. We have memories of more difficult, pain-filled times. Many of us through some miracle escaped death. We've been given another chance for a good life. We're asked only to try to help someone else discover a second chance too. When we do, we know it's not coincidence that we're here sharing recovery at this time. We have work ahead of us, work that we don't want to turn our back on. We know this work is God's will for us and is meant to bring peace, joy, and gratitude.

Today I will remember that I am necessary to others, that my life is not an accident, and that God has a purpose for me.

If God be for us, who can be against us?
— Rom. 8:31

We go out into the world each day armed. We are not looking for a fight, but we are ready for it. Muscles tense, breathing shallow, we know trouble is coming. People will surely cause us problems today, we think. Things would go well if certain people would only cooperate, but we know they won't. Some of them are out to get us, we think. And these thoughts frighten us. We are apt to be revealed as the incompetents we sometimes feel we are. No wonder we're tense.

Such thoughts are common to everyone. But we need not suffer all that wear and tear on our nerves. If each day we practice turning our life and our will over to the care of God, as we understand God, no harm will befall us. Our decision to do that is enough to ensure our complete protection. We can drop our armament and be assured that with our Higher Power in charge, all will turn out well.

I will practice arms control today.

*It is not true that suffering ennobles the
character.*

— *W. Somerset Maugham*

We've heard the phrase "No pain, no gain"
many times. Perhaps we've also heard "Pain is
inevitable. Suffering is optional." We may want
to consider these carefully before assuming they
are absolutes. It's far more sensible to believe that
our attitude determines whether we find a situation painful. We can be overwhelmed by suffering if we choose. Or we can accept our changing
circumstances as natural and growth enhancing.

If we stay centered on God throughout change
and let this relationship comfort and quiet us, we
won't be traumatized by the pain and turmoil of
change.

This does not mean that pain isn't real and that
surviving a painful experience won't help us ma-
ture and grow in our compassion for others. Suffering can be valuable in our life, but it doesn't
have to consume or control us. With God's help
we can keep it in perspective, learn from it, and
let it go.

*I am free to interpret whatever pain I may experience
today in growth enhancing ways.*

*The best things in life are appreciated
most after they have been lost.*
— *Roy L. Smith*

Humankind has made such great technological
progress, developing marvelous tools and instruments to make our life easier, that it is hard to
imagine the struggles our ancestors endured. We
are so used to these protective and labor-saving
devices that we take them for granted. We fail to
appreciate them.

So it is with our loved ones, our fellow workers,
our friends, and acquaintances. We are so used to
the help, the cooperation, the moral support, and
the love we get from them that we may take them
for granted. And then we wonder why our relationships don't always go smoothly. What if we
were to show them a little appreciation? What if
we were to ask God to bless them?

*Today I will give thanks to my Higher Power for the
people around me and tell them, one by one, how much
I appreciate them.*

He who wishes to secure the good of
others has already secured his own.
— *Confucius*

When we take special care of our relationships, giving love openly and freely to a spouse or parent; when we offer sincere attention to others, whether friends or strangers; when we regard the needs of loved ones as equal to our own, we will discover a measure of inner joy that far exceeds what we'd hoped for.

In spite of the promise of joy that comes from our acts of kindness, the temptations to be self-centered, to hurt others, to fight to get our way, still rear their seductive heads. But the gratification that results from winning a struggle with another person is short-term and isn't worth the residue of shame it leaves.

Our Twelve Step program has given us a plan of action that frees us from shame. We are no longer ignorant of the blessings that will surely come when we carry this message of freedom to others.

I will choose to work for the good of each person on my path today.

We make a living by what we get, but we
make a life by what we give.
— *Sir Winston Churchill*

Perhaps it goes against our instinct for survival to give away what we have. We don't want anyone to get our stuff. But, clever creatures that we are, we figure out that in some cases it is to our advantage. Our ego tells us that if we give in order to get something, the sacrifice is worth it. At this point a fatal philosophy is formed: what I gain, you lose; what I lose, you gain.

This dog-eat-dog philosophy, of course, brings us nothing but grief. We are all in this life together, dependent on one another. We now know that when we give, there is no sacrifice; it is all our gain. We now know that when another loses, we lose something too. We are not in competition with others anymore; instead, we need them. They are our means to discovery; they are our doorway to the spiritual world.

Because I am in need, I will give to others.

We can become anybody . . . nothing forces us to remain what we are.
— John Berger

How often during the day do we take a moment of quiet and assess our actions, taking measure of how close we've come to attaining the standard of behavior we would prefer from ourselves? And if we didn't live up to this standard? It's easy to blame others for how we responded to different circumstances; however, we are learning from this program and from one another that full responsibility for who we are and how we act rests at our doorstep.

We may be thrilled when we first realize the power and breadth of our personal responsibility, or we may be fearful. No matter how hesitant we are initially, in time we can grow into the freedom God has given us and become grateful that we're in charge of our own development.

God offers all of us guidance for a life of purpose that can bring us comfort and joy.

I will accept God's guidance as I take on the exciting challenge of being in charge of my attitudes and behavior today.

*Anger is a wind which blows out the
lamp of the mind.*

— *Anonymous*

Surges of anger may come to us unbidden, but
we don't have to let anger lead us around by the
nose. Allowing anger to color our attitudes and
control our behavior is entirely up to us. Many of
us are ruled by anger. This is destructive, both
physically and spiritually. Not only is anger a
corrosive emotion that eats at our stomach lining
and our serenity, it also separates us from our
Higher Power.

Many of us find relief from anger in our Twelve
Step recovery programs. We learn to accept things
we can't change. Our furious reactions to people,
places, and things that are not under our control
subside when we turn them over to God.

Many of us suppress our anger. We would do
better to acknowledge it and forgive. Above all,
we need to ask for help. It works. God offers us
freedom from anger, which is the same freedom
we received from addiction.

If I can't turn off my anger, I can turn it over to God.

The person who is bored in the modern world shows that he is in no full sense a member of it.
— *Brand Blanshard*

Enthusiasm doesn't just happen to us. It's an attitude that is either fostered or hindered by our decisions about what we'll bring to our experiences—from the most mundane to the momentous. This is true either throughout the day at hand or throughout our life. Deciding to be enthusiastic for a project comes easily when we've made up our mind to simply enjoy being alive.

Gratitude for the many blessings that recovery has brought even further heightens our enthusiasm for living. We all know people who are bored with their jobs, who withdraw from social involvement. Most of these people have lost touch with their fundamental sense of gratitude for what life has given them.

The power to enjoy life fully, to bring enthusiasm to whatever we do, is within our grasp. In fact, it's within our own mind.

I'll be as enthusiastic as I am grateful today.

To what extent is any given man morally responsible for any given act? We do not know.

— *Alexis Carrell*

It's tricky business trying to place blame. For when we judge someone else's behavior, we quickly come into conflict with our own. The traits we deplore most in others are those that we ourselves have the most trouble with. We see ourselves in others, so when we condemn another, we are really condemning ourselves.

Forgiveness is the answer. God has forgiven us, we can do the same for others. We are all equal in God's eyes. So when we assign blame to another, we must be willing to accept blame ourselves. And when we forgive another, we are at last forgiven ourselves.

I am responsible for forgiving others, and in so doing, I am forgiven.

The greatest happiness you can have is knowing that you do not necessarily require happiness.
— *William Saroyan*

Through Twelve Step recovery we are coming to believe that happiness wears many faces. It is a state of mind we can choose. It is within us when we get our ego and negative thoughts out of the way and discover that our Higher Power is our companion. We can join God anytime we seek joy, serenity, and security.

Early in our recovery, serenity probably didn't feel like happiness. It was too quiet, too mellow and calm. It didn't make our heart race. Our addictions had sent us soaring, and we defined that high as happiness. We discover in our program that true happiness feels more like contentment. In time we'll come to appreciate this quieter, longer-lasting happiness.

Just knowing that God is within me will make me happy today.

No one goes his way alone;
All that we send into the lives of others
Comes back into our own.
　　　　　— *Edwin Markham*

We are not alone — even if we find ourselves temporarily without human companionship. We are part of a fellowship that extends beyond our experience and comprehension. We can take love and sustenance from our own group of special friends. And we can partake of the thoughts and aspirations of our forebears, bridging centuries.

In either place, in our familiar group or in the historical fellowship of humanity, we can give in to loving impulses and satisfy our hunger for spiritual connection. Who has not heard a friend express love or speak a poignant truth and not felt his or her heart moved? It is this access to the best impulses of our fellow creatures, passed down over the centuries or heard just last week, that makes us sure there is a loving force guiding our destiny, inspiring us, and comforting us.

If I feel lonely I can say a prayer, pick up a book, or pick up a telephone, and make a spiritual connection.

Anything in life that we don't accept will simply make trouble for us until we make peace with it.

— *Shakti Gawain*

For many of us, life has become far more serene since we discovered the Serenity Prayer. But there is often so much in our life that still baffles us. There are the countless situations, in just one twenty-four-hour period, that we can't control. And no matter how forcefully we try, we can't manage to change the many people in our life whom we'd like to change. We may feel assured that they need to change, forgetting that this is for them and their Higher Power to determine, not us.

Learning to accept what we can't control becomes habitual with enough practice. And the profound relief of knowing that we're not responsible for every decision, every situation, and every person in our life will feel like the best blessing we've ever received.

Today I will accept my life as it unfolds and enjoy the freedom and serenity of letting go.

• JUNE •

To be surprised, to wonder, is to begin to understand.

—Jose Ortega y Gasset

*My obsession was all-powerful.
Summoning all my resources, I could not
dislodge it. Then three simple words did
the trick: "Came to believe."*
— *Anonymous*

We were prisoners of our obsessions. No more. Three words, "came to believe," were the key that unlocked the gates of our personal prison. For some of us, the changes that have happened since we came to believe in a power greater than ourselves have been miraculous.

When we rely on this power, wonderful and unexplainable things happen. Our recovery is just the beginning. We are also restored to sanity. Often, we are led to special people and special experiences. Peace and reassurance come to us. Once this power unlocks the prison gates, anything is possible.

I will celebrate my freedom every day by recommiting my life to God.

One of life's gifts is that each of us, no matter how tired and downtrodden, finds reasons for thankfulness.
— *J. Robert Maskin*

We're sober and clean and honest (to the best of our ability) and surrounded by caring people when we attend a meeting. For all of this, and much more, we can be grateful. We no longer have to struggle in isolation. Willing ears and arms are only a request away. And closer yet is a Higher Power who promises us, daily, that we're not alone with any situation or secret.

We're so lucky to have discovered the joys of living One Day at a Time, with the help of God and our friends. We can pray that alcoholics and addicts who still suffer can open their ears and hearts to God's guidance and love. We also need to keep in mind that the only difference between them and us is that today, we're listening.

And so, here we are, grateful and willing to help one another stay grateful.

I'll count my blessings today and share my gratitude with someone else.

*Independence, like honour, is a rocky
island without a beach.*
                        — Napoleon Bonaparte

Who hasn't taken pride in doing something
that no one thought could be done? It gives us
satisfaction to do something difficult, to lift our
head high and say, "*I* did this alone." We take
pride in being the best we can be.

But we can't find happiness in the pride that
sets us against our fellow humans, saying, "I don't
need you," or even, "I'm better than you." We *do*
need each other. And each of us has strengths,
weaknesses, and God-given talents that God ex-
pects us to use to help each other.

---

*I will offer my help to others, and in return, I will
receive the help I need.*

It takes a rare person to want to hear
what he doesn't want to hear.
— *Dick Cavett*

Accepting criticism is difficult for most of us. We sometimes feel we are above reproach, exemplary in every way. If we want only praise from others, even small suggestions for change may seem devastating because we interpret them to mean that we don't measure up.

When we create standards that are too high, we set ourselves up for constant failure. We not only cheat ourselves out of the serenity that comes when we accept our fallibility, we also miss the opportunity to learn from others when they offer helpful criticism.

Listening to criticism helps us to develop a healthier perspective on our own personal expectations. We learn to accept our best as good enough.

I will not turn from my critics today and will try to evaluate their words objectively.

An open scent bottle soon loses its scent. An open mind is often a vacant mind. There is something to be said for corks.
— *Arnold Lunn*

People can usually take pride in being open-minded. This can be a dangerous practice for an addictive personality. There are limits to open-mindedness. While we have no business judging others, we do need to discern ideas that come to us from others. There is no reason for us to believe every thought or idea that comes along.

Ours is a spiritual program based on the Twelve Steps and it works well for us. Our conscious contact with God gives us peace and contentment. Ideas that conflict with the principles of our program will come and go, but we do well sticking with the time-tested, spiritual foundation that works for us.

I will not fix what isn't broken.

The only certainty is that nothing is certain.

— *Pliny the Elder*

Since we've begun working our Twelve Step program, we've become certain of some very important things: The present moment is all we need to concern ourselves with; God is taking care of us; prayer and meditation are how we know this. Thus we have the tools for handling any situation.

We can also be fairly certain that God's guidance will influence us to choose acts of love and forgiveness in any given encounter with another person. But we can't control and can never be certain how another person will respond in any situation, no matter how loving our actions. There's no certainty that our relationships will remain constant. We can't prevent rejection and abandonment by others if that is their decision. But we can be certain that God will still be there to help us, and that by remaining open to God's guidance, God will lead us safely through each moment's experience.

Today I will enjoy the certainties that having God as my companion bring.

Love your enemies in case your friends
turn out to be a bunch of bastards.
                    — *R. A. Dickson*

There are, of course, practical reasons for treating everyone with kindness and consideration. You never know, the person you help out today may be your boss someday. It costs nothing to be nice to people, especially our friends. But this goes for our enemies, too, if we still have any. In working this program, we find that we tend to outgrow enemies.

It is impossible, in fact, to work the Twelve Steps and consider anyone an enemy. Enemies are friends we haven't gotten to know yet. They are in need of our love, just as we are in need of theirs. Our relationship with God shows us that we are all kin under the skin. God plays no favorites; why should we?

I have no enemies, only brothers and sisters.

Every happening, great and small, is a
parable whereby God speaks to us, and
the act of life is to get the message.
— *Malcolm Muggeridge*

It's so easy for us to muddle through the day taking actual notice of very little. We're in conversations we don't really listen to; we read newspaper articles and novels that we can't recount for friends; we even sometimes fail to hear another person's cries for help because we're so self-absorbed. In all these things, our greatest failing is that we miss out on God's attempts to get our attention.

Life is one long adventure in learning — learning about ourselves, and learning that true joy and security come from knowing God. No experience is without purpose in our spiritual unfolding. Our struggles, our laughter, and our pain can all be fruitful so long as we are willing to listen to God's message within each moment. And the real gift is that we'll release our struggle, the pain will lessen, and the laughter will deepen.

God will reach me today; I will find peace in every
message.

*But oftentimes if we brace ourselves with
strong energy against the incitements of
evil habits, we turn even those very evil
habits to the account of virtue.*
— Pope St. Gregory I

Many of us are compulsive. We abuse every
pleasurable thing that comes our way. Sex, food,
alcohol, other drugs, gambling — whatever — if
it gives pleasure, excitement, or relief, we can't
get enough. The truth is, though, that we don't
abuse these things as much as they abuse us.

Still, we may be able to put the energy we
spent on our compulsions to good use. When we
pray and meditate, for instance, we develop a
constructive habit. Strange and delightful happenings are often triggered by prayer and
meditation.

There's also forgiveness, which is habit-forming.
It removes so much anger and frustration that
we can find it hard to do without. The same goes
for kindness, helpfulness, and appreciation. With
our customary single-mindedness, these attitudes
can be taken to wonderful extremes.

*I will look for constructive, helpful ways to harness my
enthusiasm.*

The grace of God is courtesy.
— *Hilaire Belloc*

"When all else fails, courtesy will prevail" is a time-honored saying. And our daily experiences bear witness to its truth. It's not a major decision to choose kindness in our actions, and there's nothing very difficult about offering sincere attention to another's conversation. And yet, the frequency with which so many of us dishonor people by rudeness, interruptions, and mean-spiritedness would suggest courtesy is indeed very elusive and difficult.

Our self-centeredness prevents our courteousness. We are often so concerned with how others are supposed to treat us, that we deprive ourselves of the joy of simply offering someone an unexpected kindness.

How fortunate we are that God doesn't hold back comfort until we meet certain standards. And how fortunate that we can discover the rich rewards of acting according to God's will by the smallest acts of kindness toward the people around us.

My courtesy will prevail today.

*"What do you think of God," the teacher
asked. After a pause, the young pupil
replied, "He's not a think, he's a feel."*
— Paul Frost

If our approach to God rested on how much
brain power we could summon, a lot of us would
be in trouble. We can't think our way to God. We
have to *feel* our way there. We have to need God
so much, love God so much (or love the *idea* of
God so much) that we just find ourselves in communion with God. It's our feelings that bring us
there.

Our reaching out to God usually comes as a
last resort. It's the result of finally realizing that
everything else we've tried has failed to bring us
peace of mind. It doesn't say much for our good
sense that we have a tendency to approach God
only when we're desperate, but then it isn't intellectual power that brings us to our knees. Let's
face it, we need God, not in our head, but in our
gut.

*I don't have to use my intelligence to get to God. I only
have to want God in my life.*

When a person is concerned only with giving, there is no anxiety.
— *Gerald Jampolsky*

Whatever we give away returns to us, many-fold. When we show love or understanding, when we are gentle or express genuine concern, usually the same will come right back to us. Perhaps not in kind, maybe not in ways we expected, nevertheless our gifts bear fruit.

Many of us have longed for love and security to come from others with a promise of forever; inevitably, we became anxious that, in time, that love or security would disappear. When we view life from such a narrow perspective, no amount of love can bolster our sense of worth.

How different the world looks when we unselfishly give out love rather than longingly await the love, attention, or understanding of others. We guarantee receiving the good feelings we crave every time we share those feelings with a fellow traveler.

I am in charge of what I receive from others today. I will get back what I willingly give.

Who can control his fate?
— *William Shakespeare*

We often think we are in control when we're not. For instance, the place we live, our friends, our co-workers, the amount of money we have, our spare time — how much can we really control these? How many people are in our life as a result of our own control? Were we able to control the outcome of situations we cared about?

Why, then, should we be reluctant to relinquish our questionable control to a Higher Power who knows far better how to handle our life? Questions about our work, how to spend our money, who our friends are, where we go, and what we do — these are not decisions we have to make alone. Even when we think we're in control, we're getting guidance from God. Acknowledging God's presence is the surest way to accept who really is in control of our life.

Today I will exercise the greatest power I have — my decision to ask God for help.

The bird of paradise alights only upon the hand that does not grasp.

— John Berry

In time we've come to understand that we are only responsible for ourselves. Many of us have had to rediscover this many times. How often we've fooled ourselves into thinking that we know what's best for others, better even than they know for themselves. Perhaps the most meaningful lesson any of us has learned is that every person's perspective has value and validity for *that person*. When we withdraw our opinions as to who people *should* be, we loosen our grasp and give ourselves the opportunity to know people for who they are. We are then free to truly know ourselves and share what we learn with others.

Holding tightly to the past—the known—can shut us off from God's invitations to grow. Our openness to the unfamiliar, whether ideas or people or new opportunities, will enrich us immeasurably.

I will loosen my grip today and enjoy people for who they are. I will regard all that is new and unfamiliar as God's invitations to grow.

There is nothing the body suffers the soul may not profit by.
— *George Meredith*

Adversity comes in many forms, and it is sure to come to everyone. This might seem unfair to those of us who are recovering and trying to live our faith. But it helps us to know there is some benefit in everything we experience.

God's help is always available to us, but sometimes it seems we seek God's help only when we are in physical or emotional pain. When we were in the grips of our addictions, we thought nothing good could come from the suffering. Yet, it is common to hear our friends in the program say how grateful they are for the experience because it brought them to where they are now. God always shows us the way out of adversity and makes it an occasion for growth — if we are willing to listen to God.

Adversity that comes my way can be an opportunity to learn.

*Once you accept the existence of God—
however you define Him, however you
explain your relationship to Him—then
you are caught forever with His presence
in the center of all things.*
— Morris West

Having our Higher Power as an integral part of how we experience all the hours of a day (whether they hold burdens or blessings) heightens our awareness of the fullness of our life. Believing that God exists for us and in us profoundly changes how we see every aspect of our day. The day and our place in the drama that unfolds take on new meaning and purpose.

A number of us didn't believe in God when we joined a Twelve Step program. Or if we did, many of us believed in a demanding or punishing God who had no relevance to our daily life. What a difference it makes to let a loving God take charge of our thoughts, attitudes, behaviors, and plans for the future. Nothing can stir much fear in us when we remember that God is right here, now, always.

Today God will be the center of all my activities.

To be surprised, to wonder, is to begin to
understand.
— *Jose Ortega y Gasset*

This universe is full of marvels. No one can begin to count them. Science, using advanced technology, uncovers more wonders of nature all the time. And for every one science explains, a dozen more come along to excite and baffle us. Even so, some of us, worshipping facts, tend to make a religion of science even when the "facts" keep changing. We would do better to make a religion of what science can't even begin to explain. When we deaden our curiosity and abandon our sense of wonder, we lose touch with our Maker.

What a pity. For it is by observing the miracles of nature, the imponderables, that we can begin — just barely — to get a sense of the majesty of creation and the Force behind it. It's when we realize there's no way we can understand, that a glimmer of wisdom comes. And, if we're lucky, a sense of awe.

Today I will yield to wonder and give thanks that I am part of something bigger than I can imagine.

One can survive anything these days
except death.

— *Oscar Wilde*

Perhaps we remember the pain of discovering that a loved one had betrayed our trust. The hurt and shame might have felt unbearable. Maybe we suffered a devastating blow when a dream of ours was lost forever. At the time, our pain may have consumed and immobilized us. But it finally went away and we did survive.

We are survivors or we wouldn't still be on this journey. All of us have lived through some tragic and overwhelming circumstances. At times we may have felt we were being pushed to the edge of sanity. But we didn't topple over. And we are still on our journey of recovery. We can continue to find purpose in every situation that claims us, with the knowledge that our Higher Power will be there for us.

I will be able to handle even the most difficult situation today with God's help.

*Our immediate temptation will be to ask
for specific solutions to specific problems,
and for the ability to help other people as
we have already thought they should be
helped. In that case, we are asking God to
do it our way.*

— *Bill W.*

As much as we say we want God's will to be
done, we often find ourselves asking God to do
what we think is best. Always, of course, with the
best intentions. Who would not want a sick friend
to get well, a spouse to earn a raise in pay? And
what about our own needs? What's the harm in a
specific request? Surely we all do this. But isn't it
a bit presumptuous of us to decide what is best
for ourselves or anyone else?

Love and compassion may motivate our
prayers, but only God knows what each of us
needs to experience and learn. If we insist on
seeing things happen our way, we're not trusting
God's plan for us. A loving God will see that our
needs are supplied without instructions from us.

---

*Instead of asking for what I want, I will pray to be
open to God's will.*

The crucial task of old age is balance.
— *Florida Scott Maxwell*

Finding balance is important at any age, not just when we're old. We need balance in our diet, between work and rest, in our emotional life—any activity is more rewarding, more life enhancing when done in moderation.

Most of us developed a belief that if a little of something is good, then a whole lot is better. Had we been able to practice moderation, we would not be sharing this fellowship today. It's paradoxical that our drive to live on the edge, doing everything to extreme, has rewarded us with a program for living quite a distance from the edge.

Many a friend or sponsor has suggested Easy Does It; Let Go and Let God; One Day at a Time. These slogans are simple and yet profound reminders to find balance and quiet moderation in all our activities. We can only fully know and appreciate this moment if we're participating in it, not racing to the next thought, hour, or day.

Today I can enjoy moderation with the knowledge it will enhance my life.

It is well, when one is judging a friend, to remember that he is judging you with the same godlike and superior impartiality.
— *Arnold Bennett*

It's amazing how well we know our friends and how we think they should behave. And isn't it interesting that what we want others to do always benefits us in some way? When we are upset with people, it's usually because they have failed to fulfill an assignment we have mentally given them — or because their errors are a little too much like our own.

We couldn't fairly or accurately judge people without knowing an infinite number of things about them. And we would have to know how those things influenced their judgment. Too, we would have to be sure that our perception was without flaw before we could judge fairly.

God, of course, is the only competent judge of anyone. Only God knows everyone's past, present, and future. Only God can be fair. What, then, are we doing in the judge's chair?

My only judgment is that I'm not competent to judge anyone.

*There is a certain relief in change, even
though it be from bad to worse.*
— *Washington Irving*

It's important to trust that change can be positive even when it looks otherwise. Change is part
of God's plan for our life. Change holds unexpected opportunities and spiritual lessons even
though it may cause fear in us now.

We can look back to our using days for evidence of changes that we may have feared. For
example, we may have lost jobs, or relationships
may have ended and we struggled with being
alone. But with time we've come to realize that
nurturing relationships don't end; new people
come into our life, and we help each other grow.
We can trust that God will provide opportunities
in our life that enhance our growth, our recovery,
and in particular, our spiritual development.

Change will occur and it is seldom easy. But
we can be certain that all change will be benefi-
cial to us in the future.

*I'll rely on the Third Step if I fear change today. God is
in charge and all is well.*

*Someone who knew what he was talking
about once remarked that pain is the
touchstone of all spiritual progress.*
— *Bill W.*

It's perplexing that we don't always seem able
to live up to our own expectations. When we find
ourselves snapping at our loved ones, belittling
our friends, insulting strangers, or generally
withholding our love, we can't understand what
came over us. It's painful to realize that, even
with the best intentions, we are hurting others.

Perhaps, though, this pain we feel is exactly
what we need to bring us to our senses. God gave
us the help we needed when our addictions had
us licked, but not until we were really hurting.
The help didn't come until we hit bottom and
surrendered. Our harmful character defects
couldn't be removed until we were ready to admit that our own efforts failed and we need God
to show us the way.

*If I feel mental pain today, I may need to take inventory
and humbly ask God to remove my character defects.*

Discipline is the basis of a satisfying life.
— *Katharine Hepburn*

When trying to reach a goal, we may tire of the constant effort that is required of us, or we may rebel against the structure that's necessary to keep us focused. We often long for what we remember as a freer, more spontaneous time in the past.

It's helpful to remember that our goals come from our desire for change. We can see each yearning as God's invitation for us to move in a new direction. And we can be sure that we have God as our helpmate throughout the journey wherever our destination may be.

Goals that inspire us to act bring meaning to our life. We make progress in moving toward them, and our feeling of satisfaction and renewed sense of purpose will motivate us to persevere to their completion.

The comfort of regular conscious contact with our Higher Power, as we seek always to align our goals with God's will for us, will carry us to the fulfillment of our goals.

I will seek direction and strength from God while moving toward my goals today.

Thinking about interior peace destroys interior peace. The patient who constantly feels his pulse is not getting any better.
— Hubert van Zeller

As goal-oriented people, we are often determined to do such things as lose ten pounds, bring our cholesterol down to 180, read three books a month, spend fifteen minutes a day in meditation. We are constantly measuring ourselves by one standard or another — standards that we create for ourselves. We are so intent upon measuring up that we end up putting ourselves down.

We all want peace of mind, but when that's our focus, it eludes us. True peace comes not from trying to have peace, but in trying to find God's will and doing it. Turning our will and our life over to the care of God is the formula for inner peace. And when we share God's love with others, we are too pleasantly occupied to wonder if we're happy — we just are.

It's all right to have goals, but peace comes from letting God run my life.

Prayer for many is like a foreign land,
when we go there, we go as tourists.
— *Robert McAfee Brown*

One of the many benefits of our Twelve Step program is to make prayer a familiar experience in our life. If prayer has been difficult for us, we are encouraged when we hear other people talk about what prayer has meant in their lives.

Matthew Fox says prayer is nothing more than being joyfully attentive to life, moment by moment. We don't have to speak certain words or assume a particular posture or demeanor. We simply must be awake to the currents in our life and be grateful.

The most wonderful gift of prayer is the friendship we discover with God. This friendship promises security in the midst of any turmoil. We can know this security at any time. It is available in the quiet of our mind when we recall God's presence and hear, ever so softly, *all is well.* Making the choice to pray, to let God offer comfort will become easier with each surrender.

Today, I will seek God's comforting presence through prayer, even if my words fail me.

*Our contempt says we matter if we can
look down on another person or life itself.*
— *Ellen Reiss*

Putting someone down might have been the only way many of us could feel important. We went along telling ourselves how bad things were and how superior we were to everyone else — our family, teachers, friends, or people of different color or culture. We had a crick in our neck from looking down on others.

But our spiritual self knows that contempt is wrong and can see what a destructive attitude it is. We are all the same in the eyes of God, all loved equally. When we put others down, we bring ourselves down too. At the same time, we are short-circuiting the connection with our Higher Power.

Today I will try to raise, rather than lower, someone's self-esteem.

*Each handicap is like a hurdle in a
steeplechase, and when you ride up to it,
if you throw your heart over, the horse
will go along, too.*
— *Lawrence Bixby*

Too often we let our fears prevent us from taking advantage of the opportunities God is sending our way. Part of our recovery is developing the trust that our experiences—both the painful and the joyful ones—are part of God's design for our growth. The paradox is that trust can come only when we plunge headlong into the opportunity that's beckoning, in spite of our fear and mistrust. This is the continual leap of faith we must make if we are to discover the full measure of joy that is meant for each of us.

Trusting others may seem difficult because of hurtful experiences in our past. But as we come to see the people who've hurt us as fallible, we can better accept our own handicaps and learn from them. Forgiving ourselves and others frees us to eventually trust God in every step we take, no matter how faltering.

Today I will use each obstacle as a reminder to trust God. My fallibility will teach me both courage and humility.

*The very best and utmost of attainment
in this life is to remain still and let God
act and speak in thee.*
— *Meister Eckhart*

Many of us find it hard to meditate because
our mind is going at a furious pace. It's not easy
to quiet our thoughts; we have so much to say.
We are so occupied with this mental chatter that
we can't hear God. God cannot get through to us
in all the noise. We have to learn to be still.

This takes practice. We can't just sit down and
command silence; our mind is too accustomed to
doing as it pleases. Our first step in meditation,
therefore, is to be patient. Our mind will gradually quiet down as we wait, praying for silence,
and putting ourselves in God's presence. Focusing on that, we give God an opening. Guidance
will follow.

I will take time today to be still and hear God.

A teacher affects eternity.
— *Henry B. Adams*

We are drawn together, serving both as teachers and students, to help each other travel a recovery path. By Divine design we share this space, this time in our individual journeys.

We give a special gift when we give each other our rapt attention. Our opportunity to do God's will is here, now, in the midst of our present experiences—at home, work, with friends, and perhaps especially with adversaries. Any situation may offer us a chance to give or receive love and acceptance. This is God's will at work.

Every action or expression we make teaches others who we are. We can decide to be bearers of love, compassion, understanding, and acceptance. As we do this, we'll help others discover these feelings too. We will strengthen our own familiarity with these feelings every time we express them to others.

I will be open to learning and teaching love today.

• JULY •

Imagination has always had powers of resurrection that no science can match.

—Ingrid Bengis

Courage is almost a contradiction in terms. It means a strong desire to live taking the form of a readiness to die.
— G. K. Chesterton

When we decide to turn our will and our life over to the care of God, we are performing an act of courage. God has given us freedom to make our own choices. When we surrender our will, we are putting our fate in the hands of a power we don't always understand. God's will for us may be something we think we are not at all ready for, such as a new vocation, a new partner, a new life. It could mean anything God has planned for us.

Accepting those possibilities takes courage. To ask God's will for ourselves without reservation, without bargaining, is scary. But it is also a great relief. With the death of our self-will, the weight of the world comes off our shoulders, and stays off, if we stay in tune with our Creator.

I pray for the courage to trust my destiny to God.

I have lived to thank God that all my
prayers have not been answered.
— *Jean Ingslow*

When we were younger we may have prayed for success and wealth. But we probably never prayed to get sober. We probably never prayed to know God's will. We probably never prayed to learn how to love.

We were on willfully destructive journeys. Fortunately God was watching over us—although it was unknown to us then. Now we are walking on a spiritual path, trying to live according to the principles of our program. God intervened and we have a second chance, perhaps not the life we prayed for then, but one we're becoming grateful for now.

The Divine plan for our life is unfolding in mysterious and wonderful ways. Trusting God to guide us means we'll be willing to let the journey carry us to the destination God intends.

I will follow God's lead today.

Despair is the absolute extreme of self-love. It is reached when a man deliberately turns his back on all help from anyone else in order to taste the rotten luxury of knowing himself to be lost.

— *Thomas Merton*

The surest way to unhappiness is to concentrate only on ourselves. Nothing will bring on despair quicker than thinking only of our own concerns. Extreme self-centeredness brings alienation from God, from our friends, and loved ones.

The surest remedy is to pray, not for our own comfort, but for God to bless someone else. If self-centeredness is contributing to our unhappiness, focusing some attention on others is the way out. We always get help for the blues by offering a hand to another or accepting a hand ourselves.

I can avoid despair by looking beyond myself.

*There is more logic in humor than in
anything else.*

— *Victor Borge*

Many of us have the tendency to view life
gravely, as a series of problems to be solved. We
laugh far too little, and seldom at ourselves.

And yet many of us are attracted to the person
who dances through life, finding joy where we
would find worry; who discovers nuggets of opportunity in what we would see as signs of im-
pending chaos. This person laughs at his or her
imperfections, being humbled where we are more
likely to be humiliated.

In our admiration, we need to understand that
such people possess no magic—no extra measure
of God's love. What they do have in abundance is
the willingness to trust life as a process, as change,
as purposeful but still unpredictable. They aren't
threatened by the things in life they don't understand. They can skip more lightly through a day's
experiences because they know God as their
playmate as well as their teacher.

The humor that spontaneously arises in any
situation is a gift from God for our enjoyment.

Today I will appreciate the humor that infuses life.

*We are the wire, God is the current. Our
only power is to let the current pass
through us.*
— Carlo Carretto

God has given us free will. We can choose to
travel our road with or without our Creator. We
can make use of Divine power or not. But we
ought to understand that all the power we have
comes from God. We are not helpless; we can
make our own decision. Whether we will be happy
is up to us. Whether we brighten the lives of
those around us is also up to us. But the power of
decision, even if it is negative, comes from God.

"Let Go and Let God" is an expression of
power. We can bring the liberating power of the
universe into our life. By depending on our own
strength alone we limit ourselves. By surrendering
— letting God take over — we free ourselves.
Surrendering is no more an act of weakness than
is saying we need help with a difficult task. When
we let God's power flow through us, we are
demonstrating strength.

I will let go and let God's power flow through me.

It is what we all do with our hearts that affects others most deeply.
— Gerald Jampolsky

If we vigilantly let our heart determine how we are to respond to every situation or experience in our life and to every person with whom we're sharing our journey, our path will be less bumpy. We have the opportunity every moment to ensure a smooth trip today. By choosing to see and speak from our heart, we'll find peace. We'll be offering the gift of peace to others too.

Our heart is the home of our Higher Power whose wish for us is peace, joy, and a constant state of inner well-being. These gifts are ours to experience through the act of sharing our peace, joy, and love with others.

We never need to *long* for security, stability, or better outcomes in our life. We can learn how these gifts are contained in our own actions.

I desire peace and joy in my life today and I will feel it every moment that I listen and act from my heart.

I know of no case where a man added to
his dignity by standing on it.
                              — *Winston Churchill*

Once many of us were hell-raisers and trouble-makers. Today things are different. What a change from our shameful past. Today we can lift our head high and be proud. God has restored us to a life of quiet dignity.

But we need to remember that we have done nothing to earn it. As children of God, dignity is our birthright, a quality we share with all of God's creatures. Those who are down and out need a hand from those of us who used to be there. The love we can offer helps to heal their pain. If we accord all people their own measure of dignity, we can be sure of our own.

My dignity must never get in the way of love.

*The tragedy of disliking a fellow is that
we want everyone else to dislike him too.*
— Frank A. Clark

When we are uncomfortable with our negative feelings about someone, we may try to hide them completely or only believe they're justified when we can convince other people to feel the same way. Either way, we're ruled by shame.

As fallible human beings, we'll sometimes act on feelings that are detrimental to ourselves and others. Whether we're the actor or the victim, when our shame is triggered we are cut off from our true selves and from God. We recover ourselves and knowledge of God's presence when we make Let Go and Let God our goal.

Letting things and people be as they're meant to be removes huge burdens from our shoulders: the burden of trying to control outcomes to make everyone happy, and the burden of shame or guilt that usually follows after we've tried to force our opinions and judgments on others.

The only will that is valid in our life is God's. Through God, outcomes will be as they should be.

I will not harbor feelings that grieve me today. I'll remember God's presence instead.

I learn honesty through dishonesty,
tolerance through intolerance, patience
through impatience.
— Anonymous

Sometimes we have to see ourselves in action before our character defects become glaring enough to do something about them. While we may abhor our dishonesty, intolerance, impatience and our other selfish traits, without them we wouldn't know the joy of having them replaced with honesty, tolerance, and patience.

God is willing to help us with our shortcomings, but the amount of help we get is related to how sincere we are in asking for them to be removed. When we are thoroughly dismayed by our attitudes and actions, we are closer to being entirely ready to have God remove our defects of character.

Today I'll pay special attention to recognizing my character defects so I can learn from them.

God is in charge.
— Daily Word, *November 10, 1987*

A basic truth in our life, about which we need never be concerned, is that we are in the care of a loving God — always. And we can feel and un-questioningly know this presence if we choose to acknowledge it. When we take a moment to reflect on our past good fortunes — that we found this program, that our relationships with others are on the mend, that we harbor deep-seated fear far less often — we can use them to bolster our faith that our Higher Power is here, now, and will remain our constant, caring companion.

For some of us, faith in a greater Power comes easily. But many of us begin to have faith only through Acting As If. By quieting our mind, visu-alizing a loving presence, and breathing in the warmth and comfort, we can find the peace that *is* God. Through "practicing the presence," we'll strengthen our faith and ensure our peacefulness.

I can feel the peace I desire today through my own efforts to remember God.

We are only as sick as the secrets we keep.
— *Anonymous*

We all have our secrets. Some of them we're not about to tell anybody. God, of course, already knows them. There may be some things we consider so shameful that we can't share them with anyone. But shame separates us from God. It's a way of saying we are too horrible, too different — it's a form of false pride.

To hide something means we're holding on to the shame. Not until we're ready to admit to God, ourselves, and another human being the nature of our secrets can we be rid of our shame. But when we come to believe that we have nothing to fear from sharing our secrets, God will transform them into something useful and constructive. There is nothing we have ever done that can't be used to help someone, ourselves included.

Today I will share my secrets with someone.

The man who views the world at fifty the
same as he did at twenty has wasted
thirty years of his life.
— *Muhammad Ali*

We can be changed, sometimes profoundly, by seemingly insignificant events—provided we are willing to be touched by them and the people involved. How we thought and what we dreamed for in our youth was fitting for that time and place. But those thoughts and dreams may be too small for us today. Now, each moment calls for new dreams, shaped daily by the events and people we open ourselves to.

We're most fully alive when we're learning, changing, and growing. Not a moment passes that isn't rich with possibilities for insights and growth. Each encounter with people who cross our path offers us the chance for a deeper connection with our Higher Power. When we become entrapped by rigid attitudes, our spirit withers. God has given us life as a gift that we must open. It's never too late to begin the celebration.

I will think of my life as a celebration today, with me and the people around me as God's guests of honor.

The real gift of love is self-disclosure.
— *John Powell*

It's natural to want to put our best face forward. We like people to see us as we want to be, not as we are. We prefer to be judged as witty, clever, kind, and perceptive, never as small-minded, selfish, weak, and critical.

Yet, it is not until we reveal our liabilities that people are truly able to see our assets. When we pretend to be without fault, we come off as phony. As we discover in doing the Fifth Step, the more we disclose our shortcomings, the more people are able to trust us.

So it is with God. God wants us without our pretenses, wants to hear our secret desires, our deep-seated grievances, our shameful thoughts. As we come clean, revealing our true self, the barriers to love come down.

Today I will not be afraid to reveal my weaknesses; self-disclosure opens the door to God's love.

*Each time we sense the possibility of a
new direction in our lives, we are being
given a chance to grow.*
— The Promise of a New Day, *May 11*

Change is the one constant in our life and yet it
causes us the most unrest. We forget that change
is growth and is good; it ensures our emotional
and spiritual evolution. It promises us the blessings that are ours to collect on this special journey
through life.

We can better develop our acceptance of change
by systematically recalling instances in the past
when change, whether minor or profound, ush-
ered in new understanding, greater strength and
confidence; where we were thus able to handle
the role we'd been given to play.

God intends that we enlarge our capacity to
love, to serve, and to understand. The changes
we experience are the stair steps to this greater
capacity.

*Today I'll smile if a changing current for the good
beckons, knowing that it's God's invitation to a richer
life.*

Prayer enlarges the heart until it is capable of containing God's gift to himself.

— *Mother Teresa*

In praying, some of us depend on the traditions of our religion, others on the instructions of spiritual leaders. Some of us just strike out on our own, not knowing what to say or what to do, yet believing that form is not as important as intent. We only know that when we do pray, something happens.

And each time we lift our thoughts to God, it is easier the next time. Then, as we keep praying, we discover that we have begun to establish a familiarity. Our heart is opening to God without our realizing it. When we are willing, God fills our heart. And even though we can leave God, and often do, God never leaves us.

I am grateful that God is in my heart. My prayer is one of thanks.

When it comes time to do your own life,
you either perpetuate your childhood or
you stand on it and finally kick it out
from under.

— *Rosellen Brown*

We need not shame ourselves for occasionally repeating old, childish behavior. We stay committed to growth when we simply forgive ourselves and then focus our attention on learning new, more positive behavior. We are often afraid to drop old habitual behaviors and try new ones, but the fear lessens as we are empowered with each success. The new person we're becoming is one that God has recognized within us all along.

It's often very easy for us to fall back and blame our past for present circumstances. Perhaps our parents *were* abusive or our spouse *was* unfaithful or boss after boss *did* criticize us too much. But none of them are forcing us to react any particular way today. We can make the choice as to how much influence we'll allow them currently in our life.

I will let go of the hurt child from my past, and with God's direction, be my own person today.

The first step on the way to victory is to recognize the enemy.
— Corrie Ten Boom

On the spiritual pathway, we often ambush ourselves. We can be our own worst enemy. Or, as some in our program are fond of saying, "Our head is out to get us." The unchecked ego is humankind's only natural enemy, and the only one we need worry about. It is a great hindrance to spiritual progress.

Our ego is the accumulation of all our beliefs, beginning with those we formed in childhood, and it gives off confusing signals. It makes us afraid of failure, but it can also make us afraid of success. It makes us feel all-knowing at times, and then utterly stupid. Its definitions depend on the circumstance; its rules constantly change. But God's rules never change because they're based on love for one another.

I will listen closely to distinguish the voice of God from the voice of my ego.

*Imagination has always had powers of
resurrection that no science can match.*
— *Ingrid Bengis*

Our ability to create an image of ourselves —
successfully handling a conflict with a friend or
stranger; growing in confidence regarding our
role as parent, worker, or friend; communicating
frequently with our Higher Power — is a tool
that can enhance our sense of well-being
throughout every moment of the twenty-four
hours that lie ahead.

How lucky we are to have the ability to think
what we want to think and to visualize situations
that will bring us pleasure. God is in control of
the outcomes of our life, but we're in control of
our contributions toward those outcomes. And
one way we contribute most productively is by
thinking positively and imagining ourselves fulfilled and content through our acts of love toward
others.

---

*My Higher Power and I are in partnership in the
outcomes of my life. I know how to fulfill my part, and
I can trust God to fulfill God's part.*

We are what we are.
— Motto of Lake Wobegon,
Garrison Keillor

Sometimes we devote so much effort to being what we are not, that we lose the chance to be what we are. We have one identity for this person and another for that one. Our co-workers, neighbors, friends, family — all expect different things of us, leaving us wondering who we actually are. How can we be so many different things to so many people?

God wants us to be only who we are. We were created with unique characteristics for a purpose, even if that purpose isn't always clear to us. We need to be who we really are, and to be the best we can be, knowing that God approves because God created us *as* we are.

I will be the best me that I know how to be.

*The answer to personality problems is
found in a quiet return to Godlike
thinking.*

— Science of Mind
magazine

When we're edgy and critical or perhaps feeling inadequate or depressed, we've lost our attunement with God. And when acting the way God would have us act is no longer our priority, our character defects once again emerge and, in time, grow ever more numerous.

We can make the simple decision to always check out our proposed behavior against the behavior we know is from God. When we remember to think of God first before proceeding, we avoid unnecessary conflicts; we refrain from consciously hurting anyone; we manage to take our experiences restfully, moment by moment.

There's really no mystery to having a rewarding and peaceful life. Those we notice who do have likely made a more frequent companion of God than we. The decision to work more on our own friendship with God is an easy one to make.

I will act according to God's wishes today and, in the process, strengthen our friendship.

The goal isn't to do a successful inventory. The goal is to dig to the deepest levels of self-honesty.
                                                — *Anonymous*

The Fourth Step is the hardest one for many newcomers in the program. It is so difficult, in fact, that some of us still waiting to do it are no longer newcomers.

It's so hard to be honest with ourselves, that some of us never accomplish it. The consequences of this are a low self-esteem, which draws us toward failure.

Help is available, though. God, who knows all about us, is willing to help us get honest with ourselves. We only need to ask. Until we become honest with ourselves, we can't grow spiritually.

Today I pledge to be honest.

*People are always blaming their
circumstances for what they are.*
— *George Bernard Shaw*

It's easy to let circumstances determine how
we think and behave. While it's true that some
events seem devastating, our relationship with a
Higher Power can help us accept and even grow
from experiences that seem impossible to cope
with.

We all have known men and women who've
handled grave upsets far more easily than we
have. How did they do it? They have no magic.
Rather, they may be more comfortable letting their
Higher Power help them accept and understand
unfortunate circumstances. Once we accept our
anger or disappointment, we're free to move on
to better feelings. We begin to realize we have
choices in how we look at problems.

We are never given more than we can handle.
We can develop acceptance of any circumstances,
but our success in doing so comes mainly through
our reliance on God to show us the way.

*God will help me handle the uncontrollable events of
today. Through acceptance, I can change my feelings
at any moment—even right now.*

The worst moment for the atheist is when he is really thankful and has nobody to thank.

— *Dante Gabriel Rossetti*

We can look back on our old life and be thankful for what we are like now. Although it is useless to dwell on the past, it is sometimes helpful to cast a backward glance. It sharpens our gratitude. The blessings we experience today are in such stark contrast to the misery we used to endure.

We examine the serendipity — all the good things that are happening to us — and we know not to take credit ourselves. We express gratitude to God because we know the good things are not accidental.

I pray that I remain grateful for God's help.

Toleration is the greatest gift of the mind.
— *Helen Keller*

How difficult it is still to simply enjoy the gifts of the moment and not obsessively try to control the people and circumstances in our life. Sometimes we can persuade others to go along with our wishes. Perhaps we can positively influence a tense situation by our involvement in the solution. But we can't ultimately control anyone or anything, only the choices we make about ourselves. We can decide the attitude we will cultivate; we can decide the behavior we will exhibit; we can decide to let God participate in our life.

Our willingness to follow God's will assures us greater peace. Work, relationships, day-to-day struggles become less stressful when we've let God in. By trusting guidance from a friend, reading a meditation, or perhaps just by being still, we'll discover the peace of letting go and be enriched by the serenity that follows.

I will let others live the way they choose. Today I will live the way that pleases me—and God.

*To feel extraordinarily small and
unimportant is always a wholesome
feeling.*

— *Robert H. Benson*

There's something spiritual about laying under the stars on a clear night. The immensity of the universe is enough to put our life into perspective. It can lift the weight of the world from our shoulders. While we may feel our burdens are heavy and our responsibilities endless, just a glimpse of that twinkling night sky helps us realize we are not quite as important as we sometimes think.

But just as each of those billions of stars has a place in the heavens, so do we have a place in God's plan. Our influence may be small, our light may not shine far, but just as each star has a place, we too have a role in the Divine plan. Through God's love, we can enjoy our connection to the universe.

Today I will enjoy being too small to carry the whole world on my shoulders.

It is not the image we create of God which proves God. It is the effort we make to create this image.
— *Pierre Lecomte du Noüy*

Not very many of us have the truly dramatic spiritual experience that dispells, for all time, our insecurity and our doubts about God's existence. We may know someone who has been this fortunate, but most of us have to give frequent or daily attention to prayer, meditation, and perhaps affirmations in order to develop the faith that can come to everyone.

Our path for developing conscious contact with God makes God a familiar companion in our daily life. Our thoughts of God can remind us that God cares and is in charge. Exercising our mind in this way is not unlike exercising our body. Just as our repeated physical efforts strengthen our muscles, our belief is strengthened into faith when we make the remembrance of God's presence a daily practice.

I will remember God today.

True happiness, we are told, consists in
getting out of one's self, but the point is
not only to get out — you must stay out;
and to stay out you must have some
absorbing errand.

— Henry James

When we are down, when everything seems to be going wrong for us, that's when we probably notice that for some time our attention has been on ourselves. We may be concentrating on what we want and how we're not getting it. We might be thinking of all the ways we have been slighted or ignored or rejected, and be keeping score.

It's trite to say that we can get out of this painful self-absorption only by helping someone else, but it's true. Helping others is a way to help ourselves. It is a spiritual principle, and our program is based on this principle of love for one another.

I will remember that happiness may be found in getting out of my self.

When you betray somebody else, you also betray yourself.
            — *Isaac Bashevis Singer*

Any action or expression we make toward another comes back to us. Maybe not today, but it assuredly returns: we do sow what we reap. If we treat others hatefully, or with disdain and suspicion, we eventually get the same in return. And we can also have a love-filled, affirming life if we willingly, gladly, and honestly offer our love to others with no conditions.

We can bring ourselves misery or happiness through our actions. With the help of our Higher Power, we can sow only what we want to reap. It's a small decision to turn within for guidance. Although it takes practice to remember to let our Higher Power direct our actions, it will become a habit in time—the healthiest habit we'll ever develop.

I will experience what I give to others through my actions today.

Know all and you will pardon all.
— *Thomas a' Kempis*

We are quick to forgive our own transgressions because we know ourselves. We know our weaknesses, motivations, and the combination of influences that go into the decisions we make.

But we don't know everything that prompts others' attitudes and behaviors. We have no way of knowing if they are in physical pain, or if they have just suffered some emotional blow. We criticize many people without knowing anything about their experiences. If we were to know more about them, we might be more tolerant. God does know — and forgives everything. We can be forgiving also.

I will remember today that everyone is deserving of my forgiveness.

Conscience is, in most men, an
anticipation of the opinions of others.
                                    — *Sir Henry Taylor*

We are no longer in doubt about the right actions to take toward others. The program's Steps clarify what is appropriate behavior. Thus we know that doing any injury—physical or emotional—to other people harms us as well as them.

One of the many rewards of recovery is being free to live without guilt. Name-calling, harmful gossip, intentional put-downs, hateful rejections no longer provide the perverse pleasure of years gone by. We now recognize the subtle joy of sincere and loving efforts. We find this joy in calling a friend who is faced with a painful decision, picking up groceries for an elderly neighbor, extending our friendship to the new person at work. We no longer need the fear of what others will think to curb our spiteful actions.

Our conscience may still guide our actions at times, but as we grow in our recovery, we begin to intuitively know what keeps us on track and in sync with God.

I will follow my God-given intuition today.

*The true value of a human being is
determined primarily by the measure and
the sense in which he has attained
liberation from the self.*
— *Albert Einstein*

Being overly preoccupied with ourselves stunts
our spiritual growth just as it limits all we do. We
cannot realize our full potential when we are concentrating on our desires or fears. We cannot hear
the voice of our Inner Guide when we are listening to the voice of our anxiety. Our recovery can
be measured by our progress in getting out of
ourselves.

That's why we are asked to turn our will and
our life over to the care of God. The relinquish-
ment of self to a Higher Power is the key to
personal freedom. Our addictions are only symptoms of our underlying disease — the disease of
self-centeredness. Surrendering the self automatically puts us in touch with the power of the
universe — our Creator.

*I ask God to relieve me of the preoccupation with my
self.*

To give and to receive are one in truth.
—A Course in Miracles

Hope arouses, as nothing else can arouse,
a passion for the possible.
— *William Sloan Coffin, Jr.*

For many of us, the past is sprinkled with endeavors that were never pursued to completion. Perhaps some pursuits were more complicated than we were equipped to handle. But it's likely that, at times, we gave up the idea, or ran from the struggle, before we'd experienced the first major barrier. Then, unlike now, we were short on hope, vision, and confidence. Most of all, we probably lacked faith that a power greater than ourselves could guide our steps and help us make the decisions that would bring our efforts to completion.

By working our program, we gain confidence and new vision. As our faith grows, so does our connection to God. God is the source of hope, of all the strength and understanding we need for any challenge or creative endeavor.

With hope, nothing is so overwhelming that we can't move forward, and nothing we really need will be beyond our grasp.

I will make use of God's gift of hope to overcome any barriers I meet today.

He always lets people do what they want.
— Frank N. D. Buchman

We are born into the world with free will, and we can do whatever we please. But there are civil laws and, if we disobey them, we are at risk of losing our freedom.

The spiritual world also has laws; if we disregard them, we suffer consequences. The difference is that we are our own judges, and our consequences are personal. We frequently bump into these spiritual boundaries. God lets us overstep them at will, but what we do always catches up with us.

If we break spiritual laws, no one knows it better than we do because unhappiness surely follows. Selfishness, dishonesty, and an unloving attitude guarantee misery. Letting love direct our thoughts and actions assures our ultimate happiness.

Today I can do as I please, but I choose to be happy — living within God's spiritual boundaries.

Only trust, perfect trust can keep one calm.
— God Calling, *May 10*

For many of us, developing trust as we work our program has been painstakingly difficult. Perhaps we grew up in families where trust was betrayed. Many of us experienced friendships and marriages that turned sour when we learned our companion had not been trustworthy. And we, too, often failed to live up to the trust someone special had placed in us.

Learning to trust that our Higher Power cares for us, always, will relieve our anxious moments and restore our trust. In time we will come to know that when we're with God, all is well.

The calm of knowing our well-being is guaranteed comes when we willingly relinquish our frenzied attempts to control all the events in our life. One way we can learn to do this is by practicing quietness and breathing in calmness each time we feel anxiety over an outcome. This will allow us to trust — a bit more every day — that God is at the helm and our life is on course.

I will be calm as often as possible today, and a peaceful, trusting feeling will fill me up.

*Time is a circus, always packing up and
moving away.*

— *Ben Hecht*

We can't hold on to time. Right now is the only
time we have. It is the only time we can enjoy the
season, hear a child's laughter, feel the joy of
sharing. This time, right now, is the time to learn
something. And it is the time for us to know God.

Time is always moving on, but we can stay in
the present. To look back over our shoulder, trying to figure out how to change something we
did or make someone react differently than he or
she did, is futile. When we look ahead, trying to
predict the future, we are creating needless anxiety. The present is where we exist.

God speaks to us in the present. It is the only
time we have to make a connection.

Today I will try to live in the present moment.

*Prayer, even more than sheer thought, is
the firmest anchor.*
— *Jeremiah A. Denton, Jr.*

To pray is to surrender. We let go, finally, of
our fruitless attempts to control. We humbly ask
our Higher Power to take over, and trust that
God can and will guide our steps through all
turmoil simply by our asking.

We waste so much energy and valuable time
trying to think our way out of our dilemmas:
*Should I comfort him? . . . Maybe I need to quit this
job. . . . Perhaps I should move. . . . Is it time to end this
relationship? . . .* Like a spinning top, our mind
swirls in thought, getting us nowhere. Pausing
and turning our thoughts over to God in prayer
will ground us in the moment, so we can step
forward, our footing secure.

Our prayers won't go unheeded. Our answers
will come at the right moment. Our part is not to
fill our head with incessant thought, but to remain
still, and offer an open, quiet mind for God's
response.

Through prayer I will see my way clearly today.

When you first learn to love hell, you will be in heaven.

— *Thaddeus Golas*

With God's help, we have chosen not to indulge in addictive behavior. But we can't always choose our surroundings or the people we have to be with. Sometimes they even seem more than we can bear. But if we're unhappy with things we can't change, we need to learn to find something good about them.

It's easy to love people who love us and are nice to us. But what about those who are difficult to love? Don't they need love too? When we limit our love to those who are easy to care about, we are limiting the love that comes back to us. When we have resentments about the situations we find ourselves in or the people we are with, we are creating our own unhappiness.

Today I ask God to help me find some good in the people and things that are hard to love.

• AUGUST 7 •

*Having spent the better part of my life
trying either to relive the past or
experience the future before it arrives, I
have come to believe that in between these
two extremes is peace.*
— Anonymous

How hard it often seems to quiet our mind so
we can experience the present. We know that
we're missing God's message *now* when we're
obsessively caught in thoughts of another time.
But too often we allow them to plague us anyway.

We're not failures if we need to repeatedly
remind ourselves to be quiet, but we may think
we are. It might be well for each of us to observe a
small child who is learning to walk. She stumbles
and falls and tries again and again, often with
peals of laughter.

We, too, are children trying to master a new
skill. That we didn't learn how to quiet our mind
in earlier years is unimportant. We're here, now,
and the opportunity to practice this skill will
present itself many times today. And we will become proficient at knowing peace—with practice.

*Today I'll willingly quiet my mind rather than let my
thoughts carry me astray.*

*The first step toward inner peace is to
decide to give love, not receive it.*
— *Bernie S. Siegel*

"This is a selfish program." How many times
have we heard this? It is true, of course. Whenever
we make a Twelfth Step call we are doing it essentially for ourselves. We always benefit. God
has given us this direct access to happiness. It is a
lovely paradox that when we give, we also receive.
We are always helped by trying to help another.

Our decision to give love, then, can be a calcu-
lated one — we already know the results. This
shouldn't be our motive though. Wondering
what we are getting out of giving to others can be
a hindrance to our peace of mind because we're
missing God's point. If we concentrate on the
giving, the receiving will take care of itself.

Today I will try to give unselfishly.

We cannot always oblige, but we can
always speak obligingly.
— *Voltaire*

Sometimes we forget that we're all special people who are in each others' lives for a purpose. Our Higher Power has guaranteed each of us love, growth, and support. In return, we're expected to treat our fellow travelers respectfully and courteously. Abrupt or harsh comments put people on the defensive and strain communication. Then none of us feels the support and love we need from one another.

We can ease a friend or co-worker's troubles today by quietly, calmly relying on our Higher Power to help us in our conversations. And when we are troubled, we don't need to project our tenseness or anxiety to everyone around us. We will gain esteem for ourselves and show love to the other person if we share our words in a loving tone. It's really so easy to decide to honor one another in this way. In the process, we are honoring God too.

I will speak kindly and lovingly to others today.

*God has an exasperating habit of laying
his hands on the wrong man.*
— *Joseph D. Blinco*

At times it seems grossly unfair that we are in
the position we find ourselves. Either we aren't
ready to deal with the circumstances we encounter, or the people we find ourselves with don't
understand our problems. We feel we're with the
wrong people in the wrong place at the wrong
time. But is this true?

How many times have we heard a nugget of
wisdom from an unlikely source? Each of us can
remember the comfort of a smile, a kind word, or
a piece of sound advice from someone whom we
least expected it from. Perhaps this was God's
way of reminding us that we all have value to
each other and to God. We are never in the wrong
place or in the wrong hands.

---

*I will try to remember that there is a purpose for
everything in my life.*

There can be no defense like elaborate courtesy.

— E. V. Lucas

We need our connection to God to maintain our perspective on life. When we've moved away from our source of strength, the inner void we feel haunts us, and then, without just cause, like children who fear they've been abandoned by their mothers, we lash out at the nearest person. We all experience these moments of fear. We suddenly feel painfully alone, unloved, abandoned. We may then vent our anxiety on a friend.

Or perhaps a friend in this state lashes out at us. When this happens, we need to treat him or her with love and respect. Chances are our friend has simply lost the connection to his or her Higher Power—at least for the moment. Both of us will be affirmed and reminded of God's presence with a kind offering of love.

Each of us is God's emissary. We are here to help each other find peace and wholeness and the Divine connection. It's our most important activity for today—for any day.

I will help my friends and co-workers today by showing them love—no matter what they do.

He who sees a need and waits to be asked
for help is as unkind as if he had refused it.
— Dante Alighieri

A stranger stands alone at the back of the room. We might be too busy joking, laughing, or talking with our friends to remember that at one time we too stood there, uncertain, frightened, desolate. And terribly alone.

Welcoming newcomers, of course, is the compassionate thing to do, but it also contributes to our spiritual growth. What we give to someone in need brings something to us too.

I can give a smile and a "hello!" to a lonely person today.

*So often we try to alter circumstances to
suit ourselves, instead of letting them
alter us.*

— *Mother Maribel*

Our attempts to control the uncontrollable —
the people we work with, the traffic, or friends —
tire us out emotionally. And yet, many of us keep
trying. Some people and situations might change
to our liking, but we have less to do with that
than we might think.

It's far easier on our emotional health to change
ourselves. When we make this choice, we find
ourselves coming back to the people we work
with and the traffic and our friends with a new
attitude. Our serenity is very dependent on our
attitude. When we cultivate an attitude of acceptance and gratitude for what is, we find the energy
to change what we can, and the serenity to let go
of the rest.

God can do what we can't. When we understand, once again, our partnership with God, our
struggles quietly vanish.

*I will let God be in charge of my life — and everyone
else's — today.*

You grow up the day you have your first
real laugh at yourself.
— *Ethel Barrymore*

Do we sometimes think that the whole house
of cards will come tumbling down if we make
one false move? There's nothing wrong with
making mistakes. That's the way we learned in
the past and that's how we're learning now. We
laugh affectionately at the foibles of others;
sometimes it's irresistible. We can laugh at our
own with the same good humor.

Living a spiritual life doesn't mean we have to
be grim. In fact, increasing joy and merriment is
an unavoidable result of turning our will over to
a Higher Power. Now we can relax and enjoy life,
and that includes enjoying our less-than-perfect
selves.

Today I will not take myself so seriously.

A consciousness of God releases the greatest power of all.
— Science of Mind
magazine

Just thinking of God as we go into situations we're uncomfortable with or perhaps even fearful of will relieve our troubled mind and lessen our anxiety.

Carrying God in our thoughts means we don't have to, for that moment or hour or day, feel alone. Quite miraculously, we'll know that God can help us handle what we could not handle alone.

Most of us dwell more on negative thoughts than on thoughts of God. And our life is far more confused and complicated than it needs to be as a result. To replace one thought with another is really quite simple. A quiet reminder to stop negative thinking and remember God is all that's necessary. We may have to repeat the process many, many times, but patience brings the result we want.

God will strengthen us and take away our fears if we remember to remember.

I will keep God in my mind today. I will concentrate on remembering.

Every life is a profession of faith, and
exercises an inevitable and silent
influence.
— Henri Frederic Amiel

What we do or don't believe shows. And the intensity of our beliefs is bound to have either a positive or negative impact on people around us. If we are consistently cheerful, it shows other people we believe things are going to turn out all right. If we are consistently down, glum, and grouchy, we show others that we expect the worst.

Our attitude is up to us. We can control our state of mind. In fact, our ability to change our mind — and our mood — is the greatest power for good or evil we have.

Sometimes we forget this. It's not so hard to remember, though, if we have a daily, hourly, even moment-by-moment relationship with our Higher Power. Then, whether purposely or not, our attitude is cheerful and our faith becomes contagious.

Today I will make sure my faith in God shows.

What you are is God's gift to you; what
you make of it is your gift to God.
— *Anthony Dalla Villa*

Many opportunities for growth and glory present themselves to us every day. Depending on how grateful we're feeling, and how aware we are of the rhythms of the moment, we are able to either enjoy them or pass them by.

With a quiet mind, free of ongoing inner conversations, we notice the moment's opportunity and can know how God wants us to use our talents to meet it. While none of us can always employ our talents to the fullest, our best effort is its own reward.

Many of us still deny that we're talented at all. But when we quiet our mind of habitual self-criticism, we see our opportunities and God-given talents. The quiet left by the silenced voices makes room for the inner strength we've always had to seize our opportunities and use our talents.

Our life has purpose or we wouldn't be here. For most of us, that purpose is far from complicated. We will know it easily when we turn to the stillness within.

Today will be as glorious as I quietly allow it to be.

No indulgence of passion destroys the spiritual nature so much as respectable selfishness.

— *George MacDonald*

Self-interest is trendy. Many children are raised to believe that they should put themselves first. They get various messages throughout their growing years, such as "Look out for number one," and "If you don't toot your own horn, nobody else will." We are surrounded by commercial appeals that urge us to indulge ourselves, to yield to our urges. Selfishness is quite respectable, but deadly.

With so much media emphasis on "self," it's easy to forget that selfishness is the root of unhappiness. Focusing on getting all we want leads to the conclusion that we're not getting what's coming to us, therefore stunting our spiritual growth. God will provide, but we can't hear what God wants for us over the din of our demands.

I will take time to listen quietly today, not to my selfish wants, but to what God has in mind.

There is no area of personal challenge in your life that God's love cannot solve.
— Mary Kupferle

We seem so certain at times that we alone must find the solution to a nagging, troubling situation. As we obsessively focus our attention on the problem, we feel even greater frustration when the solution eludes us.

Most of us have heard that we keep a problem a problem by giving our attention to it — by the power we give it. What we generally forget is that placing our focus on God instead, while believing in God's love for us and God's concern for our plight, will reveal the solution quite quickly.

God's love is constant. God's willingness to care for us, always, is there to be discovered. Our challenges offer us opportunities to remember God's presence. All challenges, though painful on occasion, are really our invitations to walk a stronger spiritual path.

God's love accompanies me everywhere today. I won't stumble if I remember this.

O Lord, help me to be pure, but not yet.
— St. Augustine

The trouble some of us have with Step Seven, humbly asking God to remove our shortcomings, is that we really do want to be rid of our troublesome traits, but not until we've wrung everything we can from them. There are plenty of reasons we may give for not being in any hurry: we're too young; we haven't lived enough; there are things we haven't done yet; we haven't really hurt people that much. What are we so afraid of losing?

We don't have to be saints to please God. God knows we're only human. Maybe God just wants us to be free of the things that come between us and God.

Someone has said that humility is to see ourselves as God sees us. God loves us as we are, so what is there to lose except false pride?

I ask for freedom from the shortcomings that come between me and God.

*Some people spend their lives failing and
never notice.*
— *Judith Rossner*

It's doubtful that those of us in Twelve Step
programs fail at something very often without
taking special notice. We're more likely to see a
setback as a sign we're complete failures than as a
necessary learning experience for growth.

The Big Book's suggestion that this is a program of progress, not perfection may be fine for
everyone else. But we still often feel we must get
every promotion we try for, or an *A* on every
exam, or win every game when we bowl. To be
merely good, or worse yet only average, is much
too humiliating.

When we're feeling this way, it's way past
time for a talk with our Higher Power. How
swiftly we forget that whatever our particular
limitations, talents, or abilities, we always have a
place in God's plan. We are not expected to accomplish more than we can today. We are expected to be human, learning as we go. In God's
world we are perfect just as we are.

---

*I will learn from my mistakes and accept my limita-
tions today.*

*It is human nature to think wisely and
act foolishly.*

— *Anatole France*

It's easy to see why we never graduate from
this program. Talking about our principles is one
thing, living them is something else. None of us
achieves sainthood. The best we can do is remain
willing to grow spiritually. Being human, we are
always going to make mistakes. We are going to
continue doing foolish things, hurting others as
well as ourselves.

Fortunately, we can also continue to take personal inventory and make amends. Each time we
do, we are making spiritual progress. We make
progress, too, by staying in touch with our Higher
Power, who offers guidance as well as forgiveness.
Checking in with God throughout the day helps
us to make fewer mistakes along our path.

I don't have to be perfect today, but I can make progress.

*When we can harmonize our personal
desires with God's larger plan for us . . .
we find true pleasure.*
— *Dorothy Pierson*

There is a specific design for our life, one that
mingles comfortably at times with God's plans
for friends who are traveling our same path. Most
of us, however, have to struggle to keep our ego
in harmony with God's plan. We frequently get
self-centered and then feel confusion about what
the plan is. The doors that close and the conflicts
with others that surface are indications that we've
gotten off course. And, at those moments, life is
no longer a pleasure.

We all want to feel peaceful and we want to
experience pleasure. And we can! We simply
must open ourselves to God's constant messages
about the direction that is right for us to take and
the steps we're to make. We'll find true pleasure
from living when we've allowed ourselves to
know God's plan and have adjusted our desires
accordingly.

---

*God's plan for my life is no mystery unless I choose to
see it that way. Simply thinking of God can reveal
today's plan to me.*

*I can identify with anybody — a feeling
is a feeling.*

— Anonymous

Feelings are no respecters of age, gender, marital status, wealth, position in the community, intelligence, or any other standard we use to gauge and categorize other people. A teenage boy knows what an older woman means when she says, "I was scared to death, but I didn't know what I was scared of." My heart melted; my stomach turned over; my skin crawled; a feeling of dread spread through me; my heart was thumping — we are all familiar with feelings, though we may not always know at any particular moment what caused them.

No matter who we are or what we've done, we can identify with each other. We are God's creation, and we were made alike in love. We created our own fear, but we can return — anytime we want to — to God's love, the great equalizer.

I will say today, "I know how you feel," and mean it.

Let us be willing to release old hurts.
— *Martha Smock*

All of us have experienced at least a few significant hurts, not to mention the many minor slights that are a part of living. And throughout our remaining years, we'll continue to occasionally experience rejection, meanness from friends and strangers, and perhaps even abandonment. We have not been guaranteed a life free from pain and hurt. Instead, we can trust we'll be given the life experiences that will carry us through to our destiny.

We're learning what's needed, daily, and not all of our teachers are offering joy-filled lessons. They *are* the right lessons, however. And we know greater joy when we relax and understand that God is there to guide us through every conflict and comfort us in every painful moment.

We don't need to harbor ill feelings towards those who may be teaching us a difficult lesson today. We can see these people as our teachers, as God's emissaries. They are merely introducing us to another aspect of our evolving selves.

Today I will forgive my hurts of yesterday and rejoice that God is ever present.

*This is the secret of joy. We shall no
longer strive for our own way; but
commit ourselves, easily and simply, to
God's way, acquiesce in his will and in so
doing find our peace.*
— *Evelyn Underhill*

Joy, happiness, and peace are natural results of doing things God's way. This is an easily proven claim; all we have to do is try it. This is a very practical program. So when the Third Step suggests that we decide to turn our will and our life over to the care of God, as we understand God, it doesn't take long to see results.

When we have turned our will and life over, we are no longer responsible for anyone else's happiness, nor is anyone responsible for ours. Happiness comes naturally. When it is no longer up to us to monitor and try to control, peace arrives unbidden. And when we quit pursuing pleasure, letting God provide, joy sneaks up and surprises us.

Today I will give up doing things my way, and let God provide for me.

To give and to receive are one in truth.
— A Course in Miracles

Giving our love away, honoring someone in need by giving our full attention, will usually bring kindness and concern in return. And unkindness and neglect on our part are likely to result in the same from others. We will usually elicit that which we've so thoughtfully or thoughtlessly given.

Not many elements in our life are so fully in our control as how we choose to treat other people. There are few among us who aren't moved by another's expression of pure, unconditional love. We are humbled by it and feel valued. We can honor the existence of our fellow travelers by our open, willing love for them too.

We need to feel appreciated. And yet, to *express* appreciation is such a simple act, one that has profound effects for all concerned. Acts of kindness multiply very quickly; we contribute to a world favoring our true humanity when we give out loving thoughts even as we receive them.

I will extend the hand of love to a friend today and thus help to make a better world.

How beautiful it is to do nothing, and
then rest afterward.
                                   — Spanish proverb

The beauty of the Third Step is that there's no real work for us to do. Making a decision to turn our will and our life over to the care of God requires no energy, no movement. We don't have to grit our teeth. It's only a decision and can be made in the blink of an eye. The action comes from God.

We don't need to do anything to earn the grace of God. In fact, there isn't any way we could earn it. This grace is ours when we let it come to us. Trusting God's love for us is all it takes.

I will rest knowing that my life is in God's hands.

*Failure is the condiment that gives
success its flavor.*
— *Truman Capote*

Accepting failure in achieving goals we've set for our job, friendships, and daily endeavors is seldom easy. We often demand success, if not perfection, from ourselves and from others. We set standards that can seldom be met; then, when we fail, we're humiliated rather than humbled. And with this attitude, no matter how many successes we've had, they're cancelled by one failure, no matter how small.

Our journey is made more difficult by these impossible expectations. We seem to find it hard to believe that God does not expect perfection and does not judge our success and failure by the same unbending measuring stick we often apply to ourselves. We are successful every moment that our actions are honest, loving, and consistent with our values. And when they're not, we are successful when we admit our shortcomings, make amends, and turn it all over to God.

Today's failures will be reminders to stay humble and surrender my shortcomings to God so that I may go on to enjoy my successes.

*There is no happiness; there are only
moments of happiness.*
— *Spanish proverb*

How happy we are right now may hinge on
dinnertime — whether it is just before or just
after. It may also depend on whether we are ex-
amining ourselves to see if we are happy or not.
There's nothing like a little introspection to convince a person of the futility of life. Just asking
the question, "Am I happy?" is enough to put
him or her into a blue mood.

Moments of happiness, like creative thoughts,
pass before us all the time. If we want to enjoy
them, it's up to us to reach out and take them
when they appear. The opportunities are bound-
less, and they all come dressed up like other
people. No one has ever been happy for long in
isolation. We are not, by nature, solitary creatures.
God gave us people to be with. And as an incen-
tive to be kind to one another, God made each of
us a source of happiness for others.

*If there's anybody around, I won't have to look far for
happiness today.*

*God allows us to experience the low
points of life in order to teach us lessons
we could not learn in any other way.*
— C. S. Lewis

Today we will be led through some experiences that will feel familiar. We may also meet head-on with some things that are quite unexpected. It's probable that we'll know some fear, confusion, and perhaps even some joy today. Fortunately our Twelve Step program has taught us that God is ever present, so that the fear, confusion, and the unexpected need not trouble us for long. Through these experiences, we discover deeper dimensions of ourselves. Our reward is an increased trust in God.

So much of our suffering has been a matter of how we perceive our experiences. We no longer have to think of our experiences as bad or good and become confused about God rewarding or punishing us, or abandoning us altogether. Instead, we can see *every* experience as one of God's lessons and therefore good for our growing, changing self.

I trust that God will teach me what I need to know today, and I'll be content even in my suffering.

The more I want to get something done, the less I call it work.

—Richard Bach

Acceptance says, True, this is my situation at the moment. I'll look unblinkingly at the reality of it. But I'll also open my hands to accept willingly whatever a loving Father sends me.
— Catherine Marshall

Accepting reality is not always easy to do. Some of us have spent the better part of our life looking for reality in strange places — at the bottom of a bottle, for instance. Now we know we have to accept ourselves as we are, with all our blemishes, but also with all our potential. And, of course, we have to accept others as they are and let them be. Acceptance is a kind of faith. It says that God makes no mistakes, testifying to the goodness within us and all around us.

Accepting what God sends to us allows joy to come into our life, something that seldom happens when we contrive to produce it on our own. Acceptance also helps us appreciate ourselves and enjoy the love and beauty that naturally surround us.

Today I accept myself as I am and can let God guide me to better things.

The world is too dangerous for anything but truth and too small for anything but love.

— *William Sloan Coffin*

Taking an honest inventory of our behavior at the close of each day keeps us accountable for our strengths and our shortcomings. Most days will include a few recollections that we're proud of, and others over which we feel remorse. But we close those days when we mostly think and act from our heart with an inventory that makes our inner spirit smile. Thinking with our heart guarantees actions that are both honest and loving.

When we're harsh rather than loving, self-seeking rather than generous, we diminish our spirit. Sometimes we become comfortable with mean-spirited actions, until our inner spirit suffers, forcing us to account for those actions and commit to changing them. We can undo any bad habit, and it's never too late to heal our inner spirit. Love and honesty are the cures.

Thinking with my heart will be my guidance today.

*I am a kind of paranoiac in reverse. I
suspect people of plotting to make me
happy.*

— J. D. Salinger

How many of us, in the depths of our addictions, felt that people were out to get us, that no one understood us, and that everyone was intent on making us miserable? Most of us, probably. Isn't it amazing how our attitudes have changed? The people in this program show that they love us, that they expect nothing in return, and that they only want good things for us.

We can say now that people are plotting to make us happy. God puts people into our life for a reason. If we pay attention, we can learn something from each of them. We learn about love, and about how our Higher Power communicates with us. And we realize the value of having a receptive, optimistic attitude.

*As my attitude changes, I become even more able to
give and receive love.*

Fair play with others is primarily not blaming them for anything that is wrong with us.

— *Eric Hoffer*

We're easily seduced into taking someone else's inventory, particularly when we are not feeling very worthy ourselves. But our gratification from such an exercise is short-lived. It doesn't take us long to feel even worse from this kind of thinking or behavior.

When we expect perfection from ourselves, we inevitably fail and it's then that we may feel the need to look for somebody else's shortcomings to elevate ourselves. We think if we're not okay, this other person can't be okay either. Fortunately our recovery program encourages us to try honesty, to assume responsibility for our thoughts and actions, and, in time, to be content with our own best efforts.

Each of us is walking our own path of enlightenment, and we are learning and growing and getting better at just being ourselves along the way.

Today I will decide my own worthiness, and let other people decide their own.

*The worst sin toward our fellow creatures
is not to hate them, but to be indifferent
to them.*
— *George Bernard Shaw*

No one likes to be ignored. If we're treated that way often enough, we begin to feel insignificant and worthless. It destroys our dignity. Even to incur someone's hatred is at least a validation of our existence. So in some respects at least, it is better to be hated than ignored.

Knowing how we feel when treated indifferently helps us to not overlook others. Better yet is the gratitude in the eyes of those to whom we offer our full attention and appreciation. Each person who comes into our life, however briefly, is a child of God and deserves our recognition. Each has a contribution to make, if we will allow it — a contribution to our awareness, our understanding, and our spiritual progress.

I will give my attention to those who come into my life today.

*The feeling remains that God is on the
journey, too.*

— *Teresa of Avila*

None of us are strangers to feeling hopeless—
perhaps it was last year, or maybe last week.
Hopelessness was with us often before we turned
to this recovery program for help.

It's not unusual for us to sometimes feel we
can't handle the changes and stress in our life.
Fortunately, with the help we give and receive
from others, we are coming to believe that God
never gives us more than we can handle. The
situation isn't hopeless when we turn to trusted
friends and our Higher Power for direction and
understanding.

The paradox is that hopeless feelings can trig-
ger a far better relationship with our Higher
Power. And the more significant that relationship is to us, the more peaceful every day promises to be. Through practicing turning to God for
direction, we discover a serenity we have never
known and an attitude of hope.

*I will rely on God's loving care today, and feel serene
and hopeful as a result.*

Planning is only the ego's decision to be anxious now.

— *Hugh Prather*

Making plans and assumptions about the future means that we don't entirely trust God to guide us. It also means we think we know now exactly what the future should be. Or, we might be afraid of what will happen in the future, so we plan, thinking we can somehow control it.

What happens when we waste time worrying about the future? We overlook what's going on right now. Looking ahead, we keep ourselves from getting the most out of this moment, and the next moment, and the next. When making plans to visit a new place, we have to make reservations and buy the tickets, but we can't plan every moment of our agenda, and we can't worry about what may happen to us while we're there.

I will trust God for what I need when its time comes.

*Politeness is the art of choosing among
one's real thoughts.*
                                        — *Abel Stevens*

We're flooded with thoughts nearly every
minute. We're making grocery lists, rehearsing
conversations, or making plans for tomorrow. Our
mind is seldom quiet in anticipation of God's
timely messages for us and others. And we're
sometimes too quick to speak before we think.
The result is that we too often fail to share the
messages we have for others, and we fail to consider how our misguided words affect them.

The people who always seem to be gentle, dip-
lomatic, thoughtful, and "successful" in their
conversations aren't blessed with more skills for
living than we are. Perhaps they have learned to
rely on their intuition before speaking—let their
Higher Power help them sort out appropriate
responses before they blurt out their views.

Pausing before speaking calms us. It ensures
better communication, and it honors God, the
people around us, and ourselves.

*I will experience many moments of calmness today,
and I'll see positive results.*

*I'm doing more and more for the last time
and less and less for the first time.*
— *Andy Capp*

We haven't come this far without picking up a lot of wisdom. We have experienced many things and some of them, of course, we don't want to live through again. Even in our personal disasters, failures, and indiscretions, though, we were learning. Yet, when we go to God we often ask for solutions to problems when we already know the answers.

Our time spent with God isn't wasted, but we waste our energy when we focus on problems whose solutions are already known. For instance, we can refuse to do something that our experience tells us will interrupt our connection with God, or we can consciously do something we know will bring us peace. If we keep on doing what we always did, we keep on getting what we always got.

Today I will try to put my experience to good use.

Whoever is happy will make others happy too. He who has courage and faith will never perish in misery.
— Anne Frank

Acknowledging our gratitude for the blessings in our life releases the happiness that we some-times keep hidden within our heart. And happi-ness can be contagious. We all know people who are always bubbly, who always look on the bright side of events, who genuinely inspire happiness in us when we're around them. We, too, can serve as a catalyst for happiness in the lives of others.

Knowing that we're never left alone to solve any problem or handle any situation relieves us of much of the anxiety that crowds out happi-ness. Having God as a constant companion, and having faith that we are moving toward the best outcome for the present circumstance, makes happiness a far more frequent visitor in our life. Happiness becomes habitual when we keep our focus on God as our play's director, the source for all our decisions.

I will share happiness and my faith in God with others today.

*If it weren't for the last minute, nothing
would get done.*

— Unknown

Actually, the last minute is a good time for
doing things because it usually means *now*. We can
expect God to help us in the present moment.

At the last minute, we usually remember what
is important and forget what isn't. If we need to
do something or remember something or find
something, we will, with God's help. Nothing is
gained by worrying. And if we're making decisions at the last minute, so what? That's the
present moment.

God will guide us, and we will know the time
for action if we relax and remain open to God's
prompting.

---

*If I stay attuned to my Inner Guide, I'll always be in
the present moment.*

Truth will correct all errors in our minds.

— A Course in Miracles

The profound inner truth of our life is that we have a lifelong partnership with God. As we strengthen our awareness of this constant, love-filled presence, we'll be less able to cloud our mind with critical thoughts. Any thought we choose to hold that is not blessing someone harms us as much as the other person. Returning our thoughts to God, even when our ego is struggling to think mean thoughts, will release us from the bondage of negativity.

Our Twelve Step program offers us freedom from this bondage every time we contemplate the Third Step. Letting God take charge of our will promises us freedom from harmful actions and thoughts. How lucky we are to have this guidance in our life. Our teachers are everywhere. From some of them we experience direct communication from our Higher Power. From others we gain countless opportunities to let our Higher Power direct our actions toward love.

I will correct my thinking today by filling my mind with the presence of God rather than unholy thoughts.

There is no place love is not.
— *Hugh Prather*

Love is the essence of life. If there is a purpose for living, it is this, the finding and creating of love. We are creatures of love, our natural state. We find much pleasure, satisfaction, and fulfillment in giving and accepting love.

Why then does it seem so hard to find? Because our self-centeredness may have kept us from seeing it. Preoccupation with our own selfish concerns can keep love out of our life. We have unwittingly trained ourselves not to see where it is — everywhere. It takes practice, but we can see love in the most unexpected places, in the least likely people, if we remove our blindfold.

I will look for love today and, with an open heart, I'll see it.

*Do not use a hatchet to remove a fly from
your friend's forehead.*
— *Chinese proverb*

Some of us are prone to criticizing others' behavior even when they don't ask for our opinions. Although sharing observations is sometimes
good, we must explore our motives. Are we *honestly* trying to help? Or are we subtly putting
others down in order to boost our self-esteem?

In God's world we are equal, absolutely. We're
all on separate though very related journeys, and
we have an opportunity to thoughtfully help each
other, every moment. In this respect, gentle feed-
back may help someone get back on track, but
hoisting ourselves up at another's expense doesn't
help him or her, and it harms us greatly.

Our spiritual well-being suffers when we criticize others needlessly. The only sure way of
helping friends live fulfilling lives is to love them
and gently support them in their struggles. Their
happiness will benefit the rest of us too.

---

*I will remember that my words can help or hinder. I
will benefit from using soft words today.*

To render ourselves insensible to pain we must forfeit also the possibility of happiness.

— *Sir John Lubbock*

To be complete we must experience all that life offers. We can't escape all pain. As addicts, we know that we deaden our senses at the expense of our sanity and, of course, our happiness. The escape from one unpleasant thing often creates another. That's why we can't expect to be free of pain or to be constantly happy.

The human experience is one of balance. Whenever we are hurting, it helps to remember that pleasure is not far away. Without darkness, how can we appreciate light? Without our unsatisfying emphasis on the material, we might never have seen how much we need the spiritual. Everything we encounter contains the seed of its opposite. We can learn from each.

I see the necessity for balance in my life and pray for acceptance of both sides.

*All the good that has ever been or will
ever be has its beginnings in God.*
                    — Daily Word, *July 11, 1988*

Our inspiration to do small kindnesses for
friends, our desire to express love for those persons dear in our life, our inclination to offer a
smile to a stranger — all are reminders that God
is working in our life. Our willingness to let God's
will be felt by us and then expressed through us
is the most complete contribution each of us can
make to this spirit-filled world that is our home.

However, none of us is yet free from our ego
that, at times, pushes us to act in self-centered,
mean-spirited ways. When we aren't thinking of
God first, we often aren't inclined toward expressing our better selves. Fortunately, our program
helps us remember God throughout the day and,
in turn, God gives us opportunities to exercise
our willingness to be kind rather than mean and
show we're thinking of others' needs before our own.

With God's help each of us will share in making this a better world for all.

---

*I will do my part toward a better world today by
thinking of God during each encounter I have with
another person.*

*I have found little that is good about
human beings. In my experience, most of
them are trash.*

— *Sigmund Freud*

The father of psychoanalysis sheds more light
on himself, in the above comment, than he does
on his fellow human beings. God doesn't make
trash, but coming from someone who spent his
life probing the human psyche to find out why
people do bad things, Freud's comment may be
understandable. He contributed much to understanding the workings of the human psyche, but
little to the understanding of our worthiness.

Our program's approach to recovery from illness stresses the good. We take a searching and
fearless moral inventory of ourselves, but we don't
dwell on our mistakes. We ask forgiveness, make
amends, and put our mistakes behind us. Then
we look for and find the expression of God in
each other.

---

*I put my mistakes behind me and ask God to bring out
the good.*

God has plans which mortals don't understand.

— *Ellease Southerland*

If we had been told while we were still actively addicted that God planned for us to join a fellowship like this one, we'd have adamantly denied the possibility. And yet we're here enjoying greater happiness and more frequent periods of peace than we would have ever believed possible.

We didn't do this ourselves; recalling the past, most of us can catch a glimpse of Divine intervention. We remember with horror and relief some terrible close calls. Our stories go on and on. It's these recollections that remind us that God has a plan for our life that promises fulfillment of a destiny that will bring good to ourselves and others. Our task is to become quiet, listen for guidance, and step forward with love and trust in our heart.

God's plan for me will be revealed, bit by bit. I will be open to today's portion.

Whatever you may be sure of, be sure of this, that you are dreadfully like other people.
— *James Russell Lowell*

All of us think we are unique. And in some ways we are. Our fingerprints are distinctive, and so is our genetic makeup. Every one of us has different physical characteristics. Each of us also has personality characteristics not shared by others, and even our intelligence varies.

The important thing, though, is that we're more alike than different. And once our ego can understand this, we can take comfort in it. We are all a part of the universal plan. And our need for love is universal. We are all children of God, brothers and sisters, and we need one another.

I am more alike than different from my brothers and sisters.

*That deep emotional conviction of the
presence of a superior reasoning power,
which is revealed in the incomprehensible
universe, forms my idea of God.*
— *Albert Einstein*

There isn't only one correct idea of God. For
some of us, God is manifest in nature — in the
forests and flowers and waterfalls. Others may
see God in people's faces — the wisdom and
endurance of the very old; the innocence and
wonder in the very young. The mystery of the
planets and their orderly rotation around the sun,
that the sun rises and sets without fail, provide
for many of us awesome reminders that some*one*
or some*thing* is in charge.

The beauty of these concepts is that they are all
true. God is big enough to encompass what any
of us conceive God to be. It's not important to
have an exact understanding of God; it's only
important to believe. With belief we can begin to
know freedom from worry, and have the courage
to take whatever actions are right for us now.

*Permission for our own belief in God is one of the gifts
of our Twelve Step program. Today will flow with ease
if I let the God of my understanding in.*

A man who has the courage of his
platitudes is always a successful man.
— *Van Wyck Brooks*

Let Go and Let God, First Things First, Easy Does It but Do It, Let It Begin with Me, I'd Rather Be Happy than Right — these slogans might seem like platitudes to an outsider, but they are the heart of our recovery. We know we can live by these ideas and stay on the right path.

These sayings are trite because we've heard them so often, but we've heard them so often because they are true, they have God's blessing, and they work. That's why old-timers never grow tired of them. And why no apologies for them are ever necessary.

God grant me the serenity to live by our sayings.

Life is an adventure in forgiveness.
— *Norman Cousins*

We aren't perfect. We were taught the Golden Rule when we were young, but practiced it with mixed success. We continue to tread on one another's toes and hearts with regularity, not because we're mean, but because we can be insensitive at times.

In recovery we are learning to be more thoughtful, caring, and responsible in our actions, but at the same time, we have to intimately understand the meaning of forgiveness. Practicing forgiveness—both accepting and giving it—removes so much of the anxiety and tension from our relationships.

Our need for forgiveness does not signify failure. Asking for forgiveness brings us closer to God and others. The walls our actions often create come down when we become vulnerable and say, *I'm sorry, please forgive me.* Two minds and hearts may be quickly joined and find healing in this most intimate exchange.

I'll treat others the way I want to be treated today, and willingly ask for forgiveness if I need to.

So when you are listening to somebody,
completely, attentively, then you are
listening not only to the words, but also
to the feeling of what is being conveyed,
to the whole of it, not part of it.
— *J. Krishnamurti*

Most of us are better talkers than listeners.
When someone is talking we often aren't listening; we're thinking of what we're going to say in
reply. Or maybe we have nothing to say in reply,
but we just aren't interested in what is being said.
Our eyes glaze over. It is the highest compliment
to give someone our full attention. So it is with
God.

We give God our deepest respect by listening
attentively. And when we still our mind and truly
listen, we are apt to get surprising results. We
may not "hear" a thing. But if we devote ample
time to God, in silence, we become open to a
more peaceful, productive day. And we may see
something on a billboard, or pick up something
in the lyrics of a song, that supplies an unexpected
solution for a problem. Then we'll know we've
"heard."

Today I will take time to give God my full attention.

Babe Ruth struck out 1,330 times.

Fortunately for baseball fans, Babe Ruth didn't let his many strikeouts defeat him. He continued going to bat, and he kept hitting home runs. How many of us stay willing to try an activity when we've experienced defeat, particularly public defeat? The occasional successes or near successes often go unnoticed by us, overshadowed by the near misses.

We can be pretty certain Babe Ruth didn't define himself as either a total failure *or* a perfect baseball player. He was an ordinary human being with a special talent that he worked to develop. We are no different. Each of us has a special talent for something, but we too often let the fact that we don't excel at *everything* convince us that we're no good at *anything.*

Then it's time to turn to God to help us listen to our innermost desires. We need to trust that we have something to offer that is in tune with these desires. By merely a change in vision we can discover our talent and know that it is given by God.

I will tune in to my innermost desires for what talents God needs me to use today.

*Don't try to reach God with your
understanding; that is impossible. Reach
him in love; that is possible.*
— *Carlo Carretto*

Sometimes we get bogged down trying to figure out God. What is God's will? How can we tell? How do we know we're doing the right thing? Will it meet with God's approval? If we wait until we are sure of God's purposes and plans for us, we'll never have answers to our questions.

The Creator of the universe is beyond human understanding, but there is a simple way to gauge the acceptability of our thoughts, motives, and actions. We need ask ourselves only one question, *Is it loving?* We don't have to worry about anything we do if the motive is love. A decision made with loving concern can hardly go wrong. We can be confident of that.

Love will be the test of my intentions.

The more I want to get something done,
the less I call it work.

— *Richard Bach*

A change of attitude can transform any arduous task from something dreadful to something filled with opportunity. We can play a part in how we encounter the moments in our life—we don't have to be victims. When we're involved, rather than passive and detached, we open ourselves to the possibility for greater joy and a fuller understanding of life.

A small yet profound change of mind-set allows us to see a seemingly mundane task, like raking leaves, as a chance to experience God's presence and acknowledge nature's mysteries, rather than just another bout with dirt, boredom, and blisters. It's possible to see the miracle of life and experience the joy of living in any activity.

We are alive—here and now—so that our purpose in life may continue to be fulfilled; whatever lies ahead today can be a further revelation of that purpose.

I will enjoy the opportunities to fulfill my purpose in life today.

A foolish consistency is the hobgoblin of little minds.
— *Ralph Waldo Emerson*

God didn't give us agile minds to be content with what we already know. Our spiritual progress is often wrought with pain, turmoil, and confusion, but through it all, we grow and change. Should we stop growing and changing just because we've found something that has brought us some peace?

No, just as we test our program's principles and find them true, we can continue our spiritual searching. God has a purpose in mind for each of us, but we must look for it. We are on the right path, but we have farther to go to find our special purpose.

I will continue to search and grow until I have found God's ultimate goal for me.

*There is but one ultimate Power. This
Power is to each one what he is to it.*
— *Ernest Holmes*

Most of us have struggled all of our life trying
to control the uncontrollable, believing that the
right combination of actions would guarantee the
outcomes we desired. None of us has ever had
ultimate power except over our own thoughts,
attitudes, and behavior; yet until we entered this
program, we didn't understand or accept this
reality. And, on occasion, we still fail to believe it.

We are learning that we can't force open a
closed door, nor can we make a loved one live up
to our expectations. We can, however, learn to
trust our Higher Power's ultimate authority. In
time we will see that our well-being is guaranteed when we let go of our need to control.

A moment's reflection will offer us ample evidence that God will orchestrate our life. Many of
the times we were in pain were the result of our
ego's unwillingness to trust God's power.

---

*Today will go smoothly if I remember that God is in
charge, rather than me.*

Choose littleness and you will not have peace, for you will have judged yourself unworthy of it.
　　　　　　— A Course in Miracles

In our daily decisions, we have a choice between littleness and love. Love is something we receive from God and can share with others. Littleness is a mind-set that limits our receiving God's love and therefore inhibits our sharing it.

If our focus is money, possessions, power, to be the envy of others, physical comfort, or beauty, we choose littleness. When we choose these external things, we judge ourselves as having little value. If we care about ourselves and the welfare of others, we choose love, and with it, peace.

Every time we choose one way or the other, we are evaluating ourselves. When we choose littleness, we are denying ourselves a relationship with God. When we choose love, we are accepting our place in God's heart.

Today I think enough of myself to choose love.

The best thing that can come with success is the knowledge that it is nothing to long for.

— *Liv Ullmann*

Success may be defined in many ways. In our youth, we may have measured success in terms of having a million dollars, two cars, a swimming pool. But we are coming to believe that success means staying clean and sober, living an honest life, and relying daily on our Higher Power.

Material success provides momentary pleasures but doesn't leave us with lasting happiness. We've all experienced the rush to buy another "toy," certain an inner void would be filled. Soon, we were tired of it and looking for another distraction.

We are now learning how to fill those voids with genuine sustenance: our daily commitment to the program and our relationship with God.

I will measure my success today by the quality of my sobriety and relationship with God.

· OCTOBER ·

Because you cannot see him, God is everywhere.
—Yasunari Kawabata

*Our problem is not that we take refuge
from action in spiritual things, but that
we take refuge from spiritual things in
action.*

— *Monica Furlong*

Some of us get so involved in the duties of our Twelve Step group that we forget what we're really there for. Someone, of course, has to see that supplies are bought, the coffee is made, the chairs are set up, and so on. All these are important. But so are we. Our spiritual growth is vital; without it, we'd inevitably return to our old ways.

It's possible for us to get so active serving our fellow members that we forget to love them. We can get so busy that we forget the addictions that brought us and the God who set us on the road to recovery.

We need to seek God's will in all our relationships and thank God for our blessings.

Today I will take time to enjoy the spiritual gifts of this program.

*To cure jealousy is to see it for what it is,
a dissatisfaction with self.*

— *Joan Dideon*

We still sometimes doubt our value to the people in our life. Often we experience jealousy and envy of people who seem happier, more successful, more serene. We fail to see our own assets as we focus only on our shortcomings.

An inventory of our assets and shortcomings will help us to better see our whole selves. But it's by turning to our Higher Power for comfort when we doubt our self-worth that we are given the relief and peace we deserve. As our faith grows, we realize that we are loved for who we are, and thus our anxiety about how we compare with others diminishes. Regular contact with our Higher Power allows us to believe in our own value.

We are not in competition with others except in our confused mind. We are all unique, and we can offer ourselves to God and one another as a very special gift that is like no other.

I am unique in what I have to offer to others today.

It is a sign of strength, not of weakness, to admit that you don't know all the answers.

— *John P. Loughrane*

There was a time in our life when we felt we had to have all the answers. Otherwise, we wouldn't be admired or respected. Knowledge was the key to success, and it fed our self-importance. We know now that we don't and *can't* have all the answers.

Now we can be thankful that we don't have to pretend. We don't know how to run our life, but we know that God does. We don't always know what we should do, but we know how to find out. It wasn't until we surrendered to our powerlessness, in fact, that our Higher Power was able to restore our sanity. Admitting we need help offers us the strength we always sought but never had.

I take comfort in not having the answers but knowing who does.

It is the very pursuit of happiness that thwarts happiness.
— *Viktor E. Frankel*

Before we found recovery, many of us were obsessed with looking for happiness in all the wrong places. Our Twelve Step program has given us a healthier perspective grounded in our values. However, we are still tempted to look outside of ourselves for happiness. We must learn again and again that possessions and success don't guarantee happiness.

What we can depend on to fill our emptiness are our own unselfish acts on behalf of others. A simple phone call to tell a friend we care; clearing a sick neighbor's driveway of snow–such are loving actions that, however humble, will nurture us even more profoundly than the recipients of our love. We'll find the happiness we crave when we concentrate on inspiring happiness in others.

Today I'll create my own happiness by encouraging it in other people.

*The deepest principle in human nature is
the craving to be appreciated.*
— William James

Oh, how we long for approval. We need to feel
that our efforts have validity and worth, that
somehow they count in the eternal scheme of
things. And we need to hear it said in one way or
another. We want people to tell us they appreciate us.

How is it, then, recognizing this need in ourselves, we find it so hard to see the same need in
others? Why do we feel that other people know
what a good job they're doing and don't need to
hear our encouragement?

Each of us may be God's way of reaching another person. We may be the channel through
which another person hears God calling or feels
God's power. We must, then, open ourselves to
the appreciation of others and be willing to express this to them.

---

*Appreciation from another person is one way I know
I'm loved. I won't withhold it from others.*

*The will of God is peace. . . .When we
know peace we become peaceful.*
— Ernest Holmes

Becoming peaceful is a decision, not a mystery.
It is our ego that gets in the way of our peacefulness. When we rely on our Higher Power as suggested by the Third Step, our anxieties leave us.

Many of us are familiar with the question, "Do
you want to be right or peaceful?" We may or
may not be right in a situation that is consuming
us, but it's certain that if we are struggling to
force a solution or win an argument we will not
be at peace. How much better for our emotional
and physical health and how much more rewarding for our recovery when we choose
peacefulness over the frustration and stress of
willfulness.

We can be peaceful with each breath we take if
that's our sincere and humble desire. We are
promised peace each time we remember that we
have a loving Higher Power awaiting our signal
of need.

*I will be at peace if I let God take the lead in my life
today.*

Listening means an unhurried time when
God really can have a chance to imprint
His thoughts in your mind.
— Frank N. D. Buchman

How can we know God's will if we don't listen? If we dedicate time to God each day, interesting results are possible, almost certain. When we first awaken, for instance, if we turn our attention to God and even if we experience nothing but God's presence, we will start the day right.

Some days, if we listen, thoughts will come to us of what God wants us to do. Some days it may be just a sense of peace and rest. Or it could be a need to get advice from a friend, or to help someone in need. It takes practice, but if we keep listening, we'll be able to distinguish God's voice from the chattering voice of our ego.

Today I will take time to listen to God.

Hate is a prolonged form of suicide.
— *Douglas V. Steere*

Our emotions are powerful forces in our life. Anytime we feel at peace with the world, our self-esteem and attitude toward others improves. Conversely, unresolved anger can rear up out of nowhere, and we're caught in a web of obsessive thoughts that block us off from any love we have for ourselves, other people, and our Higher Power.

Unchecked hate, in time, will totally engulf us. Every relationship we have will be affected by hate, not just the relationship that prompted it.

We may think we can't control this emotion; certainly hate's power can feel consuming and awesome. But ultimately, hate can take charge of us only if we let it. We can always do something to change our mind, our attitude, our perspective, even if we've been greatly wronged and our initial anger is justified. Nothing need make us live in hate. Eventually our release from it comes down to a simple decision. So does forgiveness.

I will consider forgiveness over hate at every opportunity today.

Gratitude is not only the greatest of
virtues, but the parent of all the others.
　　　　— *Marcus Tullius Cicero*

Lack of gratitude is a sure sign we've forgotten how far we've come from where we were, and who's responsible. When we start feeling good, begin accomplishing things, and even find ourselves admired by others, we may think not only do we deserve this, we earned it. We think we're hot stuff.

Well, sure we are. All of us are hot stuff. If we enjoy respectability, if we are an inspiration to others, if we're in a position of service, it's because God put us there. With our cooperation, and through the love of our friends in the program, God has changed our life. Now we have the opportunity, by sharing that love, to let God change others. Our gratitude acknowledges God's handiwork in all of this. It gives credit where it's due.

Today I am thankful for the progress I've made, and I'm grateful that I know who to thank.

*No way exists in the present to
accurately determine the future effect of
the least of our actions.*
— *Gerald Jampolsky*

Too often we forget or fail to appreciate how tightly woven our life is with the lives of others. Whether self-centered or loving, no action is without its repercussions. Each of us is a very small but significant part of the *whole* of creation. This realization both thrills and mystifies us.

Remembering our connectedness to others keeps us from feeling isolated and lonely. We will not doubt our place or value in the lives of others when we remember we are each here by design, and someone in our life each day is there to learn what God has given us to teach. And that person, in turn, will teach us.

We can feel only wonder and awe when we contemplate the reality that every person, situation, and experience has value and meaning. We all contribute to life's drama and we can be proud, yet humble, when we remember how mutually necessary our roles are to each other's destiny.

I will not forget that each of my actions today will affect others, and I will act with compassion.

*The chief pang of most trials is not so
much the actual suffering itself as our
own spirit of resistance to it.*
— *Jean Nicholas Grou*

Much of the pain we suffered in the grip of our
addiction came from denial. A great deal of time
and energy went into denying that anything was
wrong with us. Many of us fiercely resisted the
idea that we were out of control or that we were
hooked. Surrender brought dramatic relief. The
energy we used in resisting the reality of our
disease could then be applied to practicing the
principles of our program.

The same is true of *any* struggle against things
we cannot change. When we surrender and turn
it over to God, the pain of resistance goes away.

---

*Today I have a choice. I can resist reality and suffer
pain or peacefully accept what I cannot change.*

The story of love is not important—what
is important is that one is capable of love.
— Helen Hayes

How many days do we wake up feeling hateful and unlovable? And we sometimes choose to stay in that place the whole day.

Instead, we can at any moment decide to remember God and the love that's available to us unconditionally. Our own harsh attitude will diminish with each thoughtful, meditative moment. How insane it is that we sometimes prefer our mean-spirited side when our loving self is far more accessible. Loving others can be effortless, but it always takes mental and emotional energy to keep our meanness stirred up.

Many of us came into the program certain we weren't capable of loving others or deserving of love ourselves. But as others accepted us—no matter what our moods or deeds—we were won over and began to believe we were worthy of love. And now we confirm our worthiness to ourselves with each loving gesture we make to someone else.

I can feel and express love to my many friends today, thanks to this fellowship.

*My life is unmanageable whenever I take
control.*

— *Anonymous*

A spiritual paradox: When we give up control
of our life, we gain it; when we hold on to control,
we lose it.

This idea goes against the grain. Even in the
depths of our addiction, having suffered defeat
time after time, we clung desperately to the idea
that we were still in control, that we were still
self-sufficient. When at last we saw the unman-
ageability of our life and surrendered to a Higher
Power, we discovered that control was restored
and life manageable.

The choice is always ours. We can lose control
anytime we decide to run things. Or we can
maintain control of our life by making a daily
decision to turn it over to God.

*Today I ask for the manageability that comes only
from giving up control.*

We are not permitted to choose the frame of our destiny. But what we put into it is ours.

— *Dag Hammarskjöld*

How will we spend today? Next week? Next year? Because the future is always beckoning, it's difficult to stay focused on immediate responsibilities. Many of us need continual reminders that detailed attention to the present moment is the only way to prepare for future opportunities and dreams.

Our specific destiny, as promised by our Creator—a destiny far more rewarding than our wildest hopes—will come in bits and pieces. What involves us *right now* is making a contribution to our destiny. Accepting this knowledge will give us the peace and serenity that make it possible to live in the present moment.

Even though we trust God and the destiny planned for us, we may still get in God's way by being adamantly willful. But it becomes easier to trust God when we see how far we've come since finding our spirit-filled recovery.

What I do with today is my decision I can make it a God-centered decision if I want to find peace today.

Time discovers truth.

— *Latin proverb*

Our program sponsors often tell us that time is on our side. We can remember that we didn't get into the fix we were in all at once, and that we are not healed overnight. It takes time.

As we heal, we will discover what time-tested advice we can rely on. We are often skeptical when introduced to anything new, and this program is no exception. We may not have believed "the God thing" at first. But when we observe the spiritual development of our friends in the program, we see for ourselves what works. We come to trust old-timers because they, after all, are the proof of this program. We can see the truth in their faces and in their lives.

I am grateful to those who have gone before me for showing me the way.

Keep your mind stayed on God, keep your mind stayed on truth, thought by thought.
— Martha Smock

When we keep our focus on God, particularly when we're in the throes of turmoil, we clearly see the path to take. No problem's solution will elude us for long when we rely on our Higher Power for strength, guidance, and clear vision.

We often forget that our thoughts are within our realm of conscious control; we too often sit idle as if our thoughts are happening to us. It's true, someone else is in control: God is in charge and has left our thoughts to us, along with our attitudes and our behavior. By keeping watch on our thoughts and choosing those that are hopeful, positive, and loving, we can powerfully influence every aspect of our life.

We generally complicate our life by the attention we give our random thoughts, but there's nothing complicated about quieting our mind. The power of simply visualizing the light of God's spiritual presence surrounding us is astounding.

I can change my life today. My only need is to think quietly of God.

*Who listens to Reason is lost: Reason
enslaves all whose minds are not strong
enough to master her.*
— George Bernard Shaw

How fascinated we become with our own cleverness. So much so that we can't understand how we get into trouble. Our mind is indeed fascinating. Our powers of reasoning are prodigious. But we do well to remember that dependence on reason alone can get us into trouble.

We become so confident of our ability to figure things out — especially in regard to other people — that we may lose touch with Divine guidance. We forget God and start thinking our own reasoning is enough to steer us and everyone else through life's bramble patches. It isn't until we get scratched that we remember the Third Step and decide, once again, to turn it over.

I am grateful that my reasoning is sharp enough to see how dependent I am on God.

*The only sense that is common in the
long run, is the sense of change—and we
all instinctively avoid it.*
— *E. B. White*

The mysteries of life unravel like threads, moment by moment, every day of our life. Each thread offers us knowledge and opportunity that our Higher Power knows we're ready to handle. During our life we'll experience at least a few dramatic changes at specific and meaningful junctures. These changes can deepen our understanding of our purpose.

It's pretty difficult to continue clinging to old ideas in the face of contrary new information. We may fight a change, even a small one, because our ego is invested in how it *was*. But within our Twelve Step fellowship, we're surrounded by people who exemplify the rewards of change. These men and women are grabbing the threads of new knowledge and special opportunities and weaving coats of many colors that will comfort them in the days ahead.

I will seize the threads of life today and trust in my Higher Power.

How the I pervades all things!
    — William Ellery Channing

If we could extract the *I* from our thoughts, some of us would lose our focus. We have a tendency to think only of *our* comfort, *our* convenience, *our* point of view, *our* feelings, *our* happiness.

What if we made a conscious effort every day to put someone else first? What would it cost? The results may surprise us, because one of the spiritual paradoxes is that putting another first, makes *us* happy. It may be hard for the *I* in us to release its hold, but focusing on the needs of someone else can bring us a sense of deep personal satisfaction.

Today I will focus on the needs of those around me, before my own.

*Love is something if you give it away,
you end up having more.*
— *Malvina Reynolds*

We've been told since early in recovery that our program gains strength each time we share some of it—perhaps with a sponsee or with a newcomer at our meeting. As Bill W. discovered: To keep it, we have to give it away.

Love must be given away too. Carrying the message is perhaps the most loving act any of us can do in the next twenty-four hours. The message we carry, that is reflected in our life, is one of hope. Positive, dramatic changes have occurred in our life. We can help struggling newcomers understand that the same can happen for them too.

We also need to share our love with the other people in our life, from family members to even the stranger on the bus. There is no better remedy for what ails us than to give a little love away. The recipients are certainly helped, but the ones who receive even greater benefit are us.

I will give to others what I have received from the program today.

*The heretic is a man who loves his truth
more than truth itself. He prefers the
half-truth that he has found to the whole
truth which humanity has found.*
— G. K. Chesterton

Newcomers to our program often find it wanting in some respect; they feel obligated to point
out our errors and rewrite our literature. Such
efforts are greeted indulgently by old-timers.
Newcomers tend to become more tolerant as time
passes and they see what the program does for
them. The Big Book of Alcoholics Anonymous
survived its first half century without alteration
for a reason: the program works.

The spiritual principles of our program have
withstood the test of time. The help we get from
our Higher Power never changes.

---

*I can have confidence in our spiritual principles because
they have worked for millions*

Love is the only sane and satisfactory answer to the problem of human existence.

— *Erich Fromm*

Being genuinely loved by someone special heals our wounds caused by isolation. We've all felt our pain lessen and our burdens flee when we're hugged warmly and offered a word of encouragement. Letting ourselves be loved and, in turn, loving others is not difficult. But our ego often complicates the process. We may feel we don't deserve love, and this would mean that no one would desire our love either.

When we feel this way, it's time to remember that we're on this journey with God's blessing. We're here by design, protected by God's unconditional love.

We're not here to make money. We're not here to raise the perfect family. We're here to learn about love—God's love for us, our love for others, and our love for ourselves.

I will find every solution in my expression of love.

*God sends no one away empty except
those who are full of themselves.*
— *Dwight L. Moody*

Simple, human pride fouls too many of our relationships. We believe we are right. What's more, we must force this view on our adversary. Our ego-driven pride demands it. But what if we give our adversary the benefit of the doubt? We don't need to insist that we are right. When we disagree with someone, we can offer a silent blessing, and feel blessed at the same time.

If we insist on opposing someone out of pride, we actually hurt ourselves. When we are angry and insist on our point of view, we are giving in to our ego, whose values are different from God's. Any response other than love comes from our confusion about what's important.

I don't have to protect my pride to be happy. I only have to be loving.

Let God love you through others and let
God love others through you.
— *D. M. Street*

Every person in our life is an invitation to know God better. We may understand this intellectually, but it's all too easy to become self-absorbed and distant. We see other people, but not with our spirit-filled eyes; we don't see them as emissaries of God who have been sent to teach us about love.

More frequently, when we first really notice the people around us, we compare ourselves to them, checking to see how we measure up physically or intellectually or even spiritually. Seldom does our first thought or action express unselfish love

We may have to practice the act of loving for years before it comes naturally. But it *will* become an automatic reaction in time, just as self-loathing may have been the automatic reaction in years past.

We can reach God through the men and women sharing our journey. It's no accident that our path is filled with people: through them God intends for us to learn to love, and thus know God.

_____

I'll rejoice in my many invitations to know God's love today.

Let other pens dwell on guilt and misery.
— *Jane Austen*

Sometimes, for no apparent reason, we feel sad and worthless. We have not lived up to our potential, and we know it. Worse, we have done harm, and hurt someone. Our families, friends, and even strangers may carry scars from our insensitivity. We may still feel bad about pain we've inflicted, even though we have admitted being wrong, been forgiven, and have done our best to make amends.

But it's okay. When these memories come, we don't have to dwell on them. It also helps to know that we don't have to hurt anyone or ourselves anymore. Through God's love and forgiveness, we are free. We can put unhappy memories behind us with a clear conscience.

I'm grateful today that I can look ahead in peace and confidence.

Man's extremity is God's opportunity.
— *John Flavel*

Why does it seem easier to finally turn to God for help when hopelessness has overwhelmed us? We get "on our knees" only when the pain is intolerable. Having nowhere else to turn, we meekly surrender our struggle to God.

It's never too late to change our habits for handling upsets that occur in our life. In fact, turmoil—silly or serious—would disappear if we comfortably relied on God to take charge of our life every moment, as suggested in Step Three.

We have all met people who seem less troubled than ourselves. It's not likely they have been spared the prickly problems that trouble us. It's more probable that they let God help them handle each of their problems. We differ from them only in our willingness to let God have total charge of our life. If we do, we will know a new peacefulness—immediately.

I will let God be in total charge of my life today. I'll not be controlled by fear. God will smooth my way.

*It is a piece of great good luck to deal
with someone who values you at your
true worth.*

— *Baltasar Gracian*

We have the ability to comfort and heal by
recognizing each other's value. It's a pity that we
don't often do that. Each time we recognize the
worth of others as sons and daughters of God, we
are acknowledging their power — and ours — to
create, to love, to make a difference in this world.

Each time we see goodness, creativity, and love
in someone else we are also acknowledging it in
ourselves. When we deny it in others, we deny it
in ourselves — and in God who created us.

Meeting anyone — an acquaintance, a stranger
— is a holy encounter. As we see others, we see
ourselves. As we treat others, we treat ourselves.
Each encounter, then, is another opportunity to
accept or reject our own worth.

I will look for value in others, and find it in myself.

*The way we think everything should and
will happen just may not be according to
God's will of good for us.*
— *Anonymous*

Few of us planned on joining this recovery
program. Most of us could only envision a life
that included drinking or using — and lots of it.
Others of us desperately tried to capture and
maintain relationships that were fraught with
pain. And the thought of losing either the drugs
or the relationships filled us with fear. We thought
we knew how the future needed to look.

What we've awakened to instead is far different
from what we envisioned. We have a life program
that is providing us with worthy values and a
loving, constant companion — our Higher Power.
We are finding freedom from most of our fears;
we have found a network of caring people. Our
faith that all will work out for our good is growing
as the examples of God's care grow more evident
in our life. Had we remained in the illusion that
we were in control of our destiny, most of us
would not be here to share this message today.

---

*I will trust my life to God's care today, and I will be
blessed.*

*I have plumbed the depths of despair and
have found them not bottomless.*
— *Thomas Hardy*

All of us at some time have reached a spiritual
dead end. We feel alone, that life is cruel and
pointless. We can find no reason for what is happening to us or our loved ones, and we can find
no comfort. And when we turn to God, we hear
no response. Do we conclude there is no Divine
comfort?

When clouds have covered the sky for days,
do we believe there is no sun? Like clouds, alienation from God is a temporary condition. And
maybe God's apparent silences have a purpose.

It may not occur to us in times of despair that
God has not deserted us; we have deserted God.
As taken from the *Twelve Steps and Twelve Traditions,* "It is a spiritual axiom that every time we
are disturbed, no matter what the cause, there is
something wrong *with us.*"

*I thank God that feelings of despair are only
temporary.*

*Because you cannot see him, God is
everywhere.*
— *Yasunari Kawabata*

What a nice reminder that God is everywhere,
even when we don't remember God. Many of us
still spend time each day trying to manipulate
future outcomes and trying to control other people
in the process. We wear ourselves out trying to
control the uncontrollable, while God patiently
waits to receive our burdens. All we need to do is
hand them over: God's presence is here, now.

When we surrender all our concerns to God —
both our failures and successes — we begin to
realize the breadth of God's care and the con-
stancy of God's presence in our life. We have
always been close to God, as close as our breath.

Learning to acknowledge God as our protector
and guide is exhilarating and eases our every
step, thought, plan, and dream. We are learning
that we can do nothing alone, but we can do
anything if we just let God join us in partnership.

*I have God as my companion always. I'll remember
that today and be at ease.*

A comprehended God is no God at all.
— *Gerhard Tersteegen*

Maybe the only thing we know about God is that dependence on this power greater than us brings remarkable changes to our life, and that ultimately those changes are for the best. That may be all we need to know about God. We can guess at other characteristics as we appreciate the grandeur of the universe and the gentleness of people who try to do God's will.

But a God that we could pigeonhole wouldn't be much of a Higher Power. God's ways are sometimes simply beyond human understanding. The closest we can come is to equate God with love. If our actions are based on love for one another, we can hardly go wrong.

My understanding of God is best reflected in how I treat the people around me.

Meditation is the attempt to provide the soul with a proper environment in which to grow and become.

—Morton T. Kelsey

You can not fight against the future.
— *W. E. Gladstone*

The experiences that will come to us today and tomorrow are opportunities to know ourselves better. With willingness we will begin to perceive God's hand in even the smallest events in our life. We will grow in our acceptance that all of our life circumstances are specifically given to us by a Higher Power who wants us to be all that we can. We'll never be given more than we can handle. However, we can be certain that many experiences will push us to grow in directions we never dreamed possible.

How lucky that we have a Higher Power who pushes. Otherwise, most of us would live far less productive, creative lives. It's not likely that any of us envisioned our current circumstances. God's will for us is far more real and possible, one step at a time, One Day at a Time, than anything we'd imagined.

God has my future well in hand. All I need is the willingness to follow God's guidance.

*Meditation is the attempt to provide the
soul with a proper environment in which
to grow and become.*
— *Morton T. Kelsey*

We all need a quiet time of day. Our life may
be hectic, the demands on our time and attention
pressing. We may plan to sandwich God here or
there in our busy schedules, but how often do we
succeed? Do we provide time for our soul to
grow?

"I set aside a half hour at the beginning of each
day to listen for inner guidance," a wise man
said. "Unless I have a particularly busy and chal-
lenging day ahead. In that case, I set aside an
hour."

We need our quiet time, time to listen to God
without interruption. The longer, more intensely
we listen, the better our day becomes.

---

*I will make sure God gets my full and undivided
attention, this day and every day.*

Simplicity, clarity, singleness: these are
the attributes that give our lives power
and vividness and joy.
— *Richard Halloway*

How adept we often are at complicating the circumstances of our life. Even simple tasks like picking the kids up, grocery shopping, or having the car repaired can become muddled and monumental before we're through trying to control the outcome.

Day after day we tire ourselves out by obsessing over the imagined details of a future event, undermining any joy that might be ahead. How seldom we trust God to guide our affairs.

Through our program, we are learning to let God be in charge. By quieting our mind, and focusing our attention on the moment, we can foster clarity in our thinking. Then we can know, from deep within, what we need to do, and what we can turn over to God. We no longer have to worry about the future; we can relax and enjoy ourselves in the knowledge that all is well.

I will keep my focus very small today and let God be in charge.

*Let each look to himself and see what God
wants of him and attend to this, leaving
all else alone.*

— Henry Suso

Comparing our own spiritual progress with
someone else's is tempting. We wouldn't want to
admit it, but we're competitive and it's natural to
compare. Our sponsors and other veterans in our
program suggest we identify, not compare.

When we find ourselves evaluating others and
mentally criticizing them, we need to ask if we
have the right to judge anybody. We can neither
compare nor judge with any real accuracy. To do
that requires knowledge far beyond what we
know. That's why God wants us to concentrate
on our own spiritual needs. We have our hands
full just trying to learn God's will for us.

*I can't compare myself to anyone, and God alone can
judge me fairly.*

*Humility is a strange thing, the minute
you think you've got it, you've lost it.*
— *E. D. Hulse*

Understanding, deep within our soul, that God is in charge of our life removes our fear and anxiety. Quietly, then, we receive the gift of humility.

The realization that we are only responsible for our own actions lifts a great burden from our shoulders. We know humility each time we agree to let God take charge of the rest. The burden of all outcomes is rightly God's.

Humility teaches us that we will know just what we need to know at the moment we need it—now and in the future. These moments that are claiming our attention now are all we need be concerned with. God will offer us every message we need in the quiet of our soul when the time is right. We can be at ease.

Today I will humbly accept my responsibilities in life and be glad that God will take care of the rest.

*Men wish to be saved from the mischief of
their vices, but not from their vices.*
— *Ralph Waldo Emerson*

If only we could lie and keep our self-respect.
If only we could run around and not get caught.
If only we could vent our anger and not hurt
others, or tell off our boss and not get fired. These
are the wishes of people not *quite* "ready to have
God remove all these defects of character."

Until we are "entirely ready" to give up our
vices, we may tend to skim through the Sixth
Step. It's similar to when we were deep into our
addictions: a thousand times we thought how we
would give anything to be relieved of this slavery
— after one more fix.

---

*I pray for willingness to release every unloving trait to
God.*

So often when we say "I love you" we say it with a huge "I" and a small "you."
— *Antony*

As we've worked our programs, many of us have discovered that we must learn to love ourselves in order to love others. However, we have also discovered that when we interpret loving ourselves as putting our selfish wants first, we eventually alienate the people we love and end up feeling isolated and unloved.

Love needs a relationship; it withers in isolation. We must allow ourselves to both give and feel love — within ourselves, with God, and other people. And when we withdraw our ego's self-will from the moment, love can freely flow from within and come back to us from other people and God. We receive, in full measure, that which we give.

I will offer love today, fully and freely, and will be open to its return.

It is impossible on reasonable grounds to disbelieve miracles.

— *Blaise Pascal*

We who have entrusted our life to a Higher Power can tell of strange and wonderful happenings. Unexplainable though they may be, they often come dressed in ordinary clothes. Yet there is something about these moments that doesn't seem ordinary. Something is a bit out of sync with time or place. Something unusual. And we can't suppress a little shiver.

We can credit some happenings to coincidence. After all, everyone is entitled to serendipity now and then. But when good things begin multiplying, we have to face it — somebody's trying to tell us something. And we recall that it all began shortly after we took the Third Step.

How can I not believe in miracles? I am a miracle.

*Example moves the world more than
doctrine.*
— *Henry Miller*

We may have come to this program because
we were given an ultimatum. But we stayed because we liked what we saw in others. Now by
our example other men and women are attracted
to this way of life.

It is human nature to observe others and imitate behaviors that seem appealing. We did it
when we were young. Unfortunately, we often
decided to imitate unhealthy habits along with
healthy ones. In fact, most of us got into the program after years of unhealthy imitations. We now
have opportunities to imitate behaviors that are
spirit-filled, that will enhance our sober life, and
that will foster our personal growth.

Offering good examples of behavior to others
is rewarding in very personal ways. It helps us
stay committed to the program, and it becomes a
valued habit, one that's guaranteed to carry us
more sanely and securely into the days ahead.

*Today I will be conscious of the example I'm setting
for others. I will strive to demonstrate spirit-filled
behavior.*

God's will is not an itinerary but an attitude.

— *Andrew Dhuse*

When we make the decision to turn our will over to the care of God, what are we actually doing? We're asking God to be our personal manager. We are saying, "Please, you manage my money, my home, my children, my friends, my job." And we leave nothing out. Our secret thoughts, our health, our longings, our fears — we turn them all over to our manager's care. Since we have no way of knowing the ultimate consequences of our own decisions, we are saying, "You decide."

And then something miraculous happens. Peace descends upon us. It comes when we take the attitude that there is not a single part of our life, not the least idle wish, that we can handle as well as our manager.

My attitude today is that I can ask for help with every aspect of living.

To speak ill of others is a dishonest way of praising ourselves.
— *Will Durant*

In our youth many of us heard from our mother or father, "If you can't say anything nice about someone, don't say anything at all." We didn't practice this principle very well then, and many of us still don't. The real root of our struggle to speak well of others is the pain we suffer because of our low self-esteem, and diminishing another person's worth, unfortunately, gives us a moment of stolen satisfaction. But in reality, the illusion of elevating our own worth for that brief, hurtful moment dies quickly, and our remorse and shame linger on.

In God's eyes, we are all equal. To God, no one among us has more value than another.

Praying for knowledge of this understanding every day will relieve our compulsion to diminish someone else. And even more importantly, it will help us understand our equality and value in this living universe.

I will see worth and value in myself and everyone else today.

*All the troubles of life come upon us
because we refuse to sit quietly for awhile
each day in our rooms.*
— *Blaise Pascal*

It's hard to believe that just sitting and listening to God can change the character of our day. Remembering the words "Be still and know that I am God" can brighten our day, sometimes even producing startling results. Difficult encounters are made easy, problems solved, goals met, relationships improved.

When we find ourselves too busy to take time for God, things go wrong — not because God is punishing us, but because when we are on our own, we are at our worst. It's always our choice.

Listening to God, sensing the presence of God — something we can do just by wanting it — makes a difference in the quality of our day. And we don't have to take anyone's word for it. We can try it for ourselves, on any day we choose.

I will start today right, in the presence of my Higher Power.

We never know the worth of water till the well is dry.

— *English proverb*

Every moment that passes us by unnoticed is a lost gift: the stranger's smile to acknowledge us; the friend's hug to comfort us; the rainbow's brilliance just beyond the bend in the road. These are all gifts from our Creator, meant to bless and connect us to one another and the world. These gifts enhance our growth and nourish our spirit.

It's easy to wear blinders. Self-absorption, which is all too familiar to many of us, keeps us in a quagmire that stifles us. We cannot give or receive the gifts of our Creator when we're self-absorbed. The connection between us and our companions is severed each time we become self-centered. Restoring that connection is as simple as shifting our attention to someone in need.

A gift from God awaits us.

I am in the company of people who are important to me every day. Let me notice them today and receive God's blessing.

A little lifting of the heart suffices; a little remembrance of God, one act of inward worship are prayers which, however short, are nevertheless acceptable to God.
— *Brother Lawrence*

Our days are filled with busyness. Few of us seem to have time to pause for a breath of fresh air, let alone take time out to commune with our Higher Power. But if we practice knowing that God is present in our life, and keep at it until it becomes habitual, we find ourselves noticing that we are not alone.

And it doesn't take much to establish a connection. Just thinking that God cares is enough to do it. Realizing that we can commune with God through other people does it too. A smile, a sympathetic word, a pat on the back, and we are connected.

I will practice sensing God in all that I do and in everyone I meet.

*Be of love a little more careful than of
anything.*

— *e. e. cummings*

Life's assignment is to live unselfishly, lovingly, and cooperatively with God's will. The
program's principles, which are offered as guidance for our life, make our assignment quite
manageable — even simple. It's often only a
matter of expressing the love we feel to the people
who cross our path each day. Our own burdens
will lighten every time we show kindness to another person. Our conflicts mysteriously begin to
dissipate when we switch from a fearful, negative
outlook to a loving, trusting one.

Love is God's gift, and our existence is proof of
that love. When we offer love freely and honestly
to someone else, we give a gift not only to that
person by showing unconditional love, but also
to God by doing God's will. We also give a gift to
ourselves in that each expression of love heightens
our own awareness of being loved.

I will share and receive many gifts of love today.

*Doubt is a pain too lonely to know that
faith is his twin brother.*
— *Kahlil Gibran*

People who say their faith is unshakable are
apt to be fudging. Few of us, even the most devout,
have gone unquestioning through all life's tribu-
lations. Some of us, in fact, find our faith in God
wavering even in good times.

Erich Fromm calls doubt "the fertile condition
of all progress," and Malcolm Muggeridge goes
so far as to call it "an integral part of coming to
have faith." How could there be faith without
doubt, or doubt without faith? They are different
sides of the same coin, both part of being human.

So we need never feel ashamed of our doubts.
They mean we are still searching. This searching,
to Blaise Pascal, is synonymous to finding: "You
would not be looking for Me if you did not possess Me."

*Today I am grateful for my doubts; they keep me in
touch with God.*

*Life is what happens to us while we're
making other plans.*
— William Gaddis

It's easy to let our mind dwell on the future.
We may take great pride in being well-organized
and able to plan ahead. It's certainly no short-
coming to plan ahead in some instances; many
things in life require careful planning. But we can
get so focused on planning, that the very life
we're given *right now* goes unnoticed.

Each moment is precious, never to return.
Whatever we might experience in each moment
will not come to us in just that particular way
ever again.

We're the losers when we check out on *now* and
live in the past or future instead. We can check
back in, however, just as quickly as we wandered
off. We may need to keep reminding ourselves
not to let life pass us by, but with practice, living
in the present can become as natural as breathing.

---

*I will remind myself that the moment I'm in is the best
part of today.*

*All men who live with any degree of
serenity live with some assurance of
grace.*

— *Reinhold Niebuhr*

Grace is God's unmerited love. It is Divine
help we did nothing to deserve. It is, in fact, the
proof of God's love. We all know our behavior is
less than perfect. Yet God sees us as perfect. God
overlooks our mistakes and reassures us. Nothing we have done or will ever do can alter that
grace. Although we have not earned it, it is ours.

That takes some getting used to. For most of
our life we were convinced that we were in trouble
with God, if there even was a God. Now, in this
program, we are in trouble with no one, least of
all the God who has restored us to sanity. If we
have any doubt about that, it recedes as we practice the same forgiveness we have received.

*My serenity comes from knowing that I am loved
whether I deserve it or not.*

We must not . . . ignore the small daily differences we can make which, over time, add up to big differences that we often cannot foresee.
— *Marian Wright Edelman*

It's a healthy human attribute to want our life to count. But some of us immediately picture people like Mother Teresa, Albert Einstein, Martin Luther King, and we think we could never measure up. What we fail to realize is that their successes really grew from many small steps, and even some stumbles.

Thomas Edison made thousands of attempts before he invented the first successful light bulb. He wasn't diminished by each failure. It has been said that he was inspired because he knew he was drawing closer to success each time by the process of elimination.

The same philosophy can work for us. Each failure or rejection can bring us one step closer to our true goal. And giving genuine love to others ensures that our life is counting in the most meaningful way of all.

Today, I'll remember three things: I count; I am alive for a purpose; I am made to give and receive love.

The deepest need of man is the need to overcome his separateness, to leave the prison of his aloneness.

— *Erich Fromm*

Some of us are instinctively shy by nature; we may even seem standoffish. Then our addictions made loners of many of us. Even those of us who are gregarious could find ourselves lonely in a crowd. And we all can agree that feeling alone can be wretched. God did not make us to stand apart.

Our program has revealed to us that a deep sense of fulfillment can come from helping others. It is the warmth of being with our brothers and sisters, intent on a common purpose, that shows us by contrast how cold and desolate separation is. We need each other, just as we need God.

I am not alone.

Grumbling is the death of love.
            — Marlene Dietrich

This moment is all we're promised. Many moments will fall short of our expectations, yet the problem never lies in the moment itself, but in our expectations.

We are easier on ourselves and our loved ones when we adjust our attitude to one of gratefulness — being grateful for each moment. Incessant grumbling drives people away; it blocks the flow of love from us to them and inhibits them from showing their love for us.

Grumbling can be habit forming. Unfortunately, it can also be human forming; where grumbling prevails, love is neither given nor received, and our true nature, our purpose for living, is lost.

It's easy to forget that each moment is given as an opportunity to love ourselves and one another. When we pay attention to the moment, we notice that it takes far less energy to love than to grumble.

I don't need to grumble today. Instead, I will make the decision to feel grateful and share my gratitude with others

*I am not a body. I am free. For I am still
as God created me.*
— A Course in Miracles

When we think of ourselves and others as only physical beings, we are limiting our ability to know one another. And we are limiting ourselves. We may be putting too much faith in the looks and condition of our body, thinking that when it fails us, we fail.

We spend great amounts of time planning for the comfort, protection, and enjoyment of our body. Yet we are not just a body. Our natural state is that of a loving spirit.

Our body is outside us, seeming to surround us, keeping us separate from others. But there is no physical barrier between God and us; and the physical barrier between God's sons and daughters is only an illusion — one created by the value we put on our body. When we look at each other, not with our eyes, but with love and forgiveness, the barriers drop and we communicate spirit to spirit.

Today I will look beyond my body to find a loving spirit.

Out of our beliefs are born deeds; out of our deeds we form habits; out of our habits grows our character.
— Henry Hancock

Over others we are powerless. Over who we are this moment, and who we are intent on becoming, we have vast power. We can take this power in hand and form ourselves as persons short on character defects and long on positive assets. Or, we can sit idle, feeling sorry for ourselves, waiting for someone else to change us or for the circumstances of our life to change.

God has given us free will to mold ourselves. This program has given us the tools to become the people we'd like to be. The rest is up to us. Our mind is formed largely by what we put into it. Our actions are ours to own. No one can act for us, and we no longer need to behave in ways that conflict with our best interests and values. Our character is never wholly forced upon us. We can be, to a large extent, who we intend to be. It's our responsibility, through our Higher Power, to determine our intentions.

Today my words and actions will reflect who I really want to be.

Hesitation is the best cure for anger. . . .
The first blows of anger are heavy, but if
it waits, it will think again.

— Seneca

Everybody knows that expressing anger dissipates it, right? Not always. Just the opposite can be true — anger feeds on itself. We've seen that for ourselves, when we've vented our anger and actually grown more angry, not less.

We can handle our anger sensibly. If someone's words, actions, or attitudes have offended us, we help both ourselves and the other person by making peace. God is all-forgiving; it is our challenge to be forgiving too.

Instead of getting angry, I pray that I'll make peace and forgive.

Love life for better or worse without conditions.
— *Arthur Rubinstein*

Not everything that happens today will bring us joy, and it's unlikely that we'll be completely peaceful throughout the next twenty-four hours either. A morning traffic jam or an angry boss may be enough to ruin our whole day.

But we can retain our serenity through every experience, if that's our choice. We can decide to accept each circumstance, embrace each moment, and be grateful to God for our life. We can see our struggles as lessons we need to learn.

We can often learn more from hard times than from periods of calm. Our struggles force us to gather our resources and help us shift our focus back to our Higher Power for guidance and comfort. We'll regain our sense of gratitude when our blessings are brought back into focus.

Making the decision to accept life as it comes promises us comfort and freedom from worry. We are in God's care, and this life is God's most precious gift to us.

I will relax and trust that God is accompanying me through every experience today.

Be not afraid of growing slowly, be afraid only of standing still.

— *Chinese proverb*

Many of us are dissatisfied with our progress. Our mind is clear and we're in touch with our feelings. We have friends to talk to and useful things to do. Why, then, are we so unhappy at times? We look at others growing confident and prosperous. Why not us?

Our growth rate is not up to us. Maybe we have more character defects to overcome. Maybe God has special things for us to learn, and it's taking time. Slow progress means we're learning our lessons well. And any progress is better than none. In fact, when we make no progress, we don't stand still — we slip backward. As long as we're in touch with God and sharing our love with others, we're advancing. And, according to God's schedule, we're on time.

I'm grateful to God that I'm growing, however slow.

Bitterness imprisons life; love releases it.
— Harry Emerson Fosdick

Mean-spiritedness poisons us and our relationships. In time, hatefulness erects tall walls around us, walls that grow taller and creep closer to us with each passing day. These walls imprison us by keeping others away and keeping us from knowing God's love.

Most of us come to know God and feel God's love through other people. Through our relationships with others, we learn what our life is about and we grow. If we erect walls of isolation, our life is reduced to but a shadow of what our Higher Power intended. But our isolation affects more than our own life. It affects everyone traveling on our path. By being present in other people's lives, we can teach them what we know about life and they, in turn, can help us grow.

When we take down our walls, we discover how necessary we are to one another, and to God.

I will tear down the walls of mean-spiritedness and express my loving spirit today.

*Anxiety is the natural result when our
hopes are centered in anything short of
God and his will for us.*

— Billy Graham

When we've embarked on a spiritual path, trying to learn the will of God seems essential to our
peace of mind. And peace of mind is what we all
want.

As we try on a daily basis to improve our
conscious contact with God, praying for knowledge of God's will for us, we sometimes find
ourselves doing things we never thought we'd
do. We may find we're more loving; we treat
others as equals; we're more consistently kind,
gentle, and considerate. We may begin forgiving
others, just as God does us, and find that we
catch a glimpse of God in everyone we see. And
then we just may discover we are surprisingly
free of anxiety.

---

*Today I will seek God's will for me and look for oppor-
tunities to express it.*

Envy is a kind of praise.

— *John Gay*

Since our introduction to this program, we have probably revised our list of people whom we envy. In the past, those who were on our list were probably there because of their external appearances.

We've since come to admire men and women who clearly walk a spiritual path on a daily basis. We appreciate how they openly share their journey and rely on God. The program has taught us to want our inner life to resemble their inner life We can see, now, that people who are God-centered rather than ego-centered really have personal qualities worth envying. We'll find what we're looking for among these friends.

I will emulate God-centered people today.

We are all serving a life sentence in the dungeon of self.

— *Cyril Connolly*

Some say the whole purpose of our sojourn here is to escape from self. It is gloomy and frightening in that private inner dungeon. Many of us have tried to escape, hoping that when we came to our senses we would no longer be a prisoner. Thankfully, our addictions brought us to our knees in defeat — and we had to acknowledge a power greater than ourselves. It was the only way some of us might have ever known God.

Those of us who feel a Guiding Hand in our life know that we escape ourselves by getting involved with others. The bars of self crumble as we become honest and share our fears and weaknesses, hopes and strengths with each other.

Today I will look for opportunities to share my inner self.

• DECEMBER •

I would rather live in a world where my life is surrounded by mystery than live in a world so small that my mind could comprehend it.
—Henry Emerson Fosdick

Don't forget to love yourself.
— *Soren Kierkegaard*

Kierkegaard's statement is so straightforward that it sounds like loving ourselves is only a matter of making a simple decision. And yet we've all had to struggle to love ourselves at times, so many of us failing far too often. Still bound by shame, we often found anger or fear much easier. But by working our Twelve Step program, we're discovering our ability to love and learning how it feels to be loved.

We often hear it said that we must love ourselves before we can love others. But any act of love expands our ability to both give and receive it. Love is a decision, one that means nothing more at times than a willingness to be more gentle with others and ourselves. This is a far easier response to any moment than the anger and fear that have so often consumed us.

Observing life through loving eyes, and experiencing life with a heart that holds only love, promise a richness to the tapestry of our life that we would have never imagined.

I will decide for gentle, loving thoughts today.

It is as absurd to argue men, as to torture them, into believing.
— *John Henry Newman*

We don't come to our beliefs by persuasion but by experience. The suggestions we are given in our Twelve Step program don't mean as much to us until we put them into practice. Then our circumstances and attitudes begin changing.

We come to our belief that God can help us in the same way. Many of us are skeptical of giving up control of our lives; we may not believe that we can or that we should. But just going through the motions of turning our will over to a Higher Power often brings surprising and dramatic results. A little willingness is all it takes.

I will put the spiritual ideas I am given into practice.

*It is the heart which experiences God and
not the reason.*

— Blaise Pascal

In symbolic terms, our heart is where our
Higher Power resides, and our mind is where our
logic resides. Sometimes it might be easier to pay
attention to our mind's messages than to our
heart's, but we're learning that our mind and our
heart must work compatibly to allow our friendship with God to grow. The more we rely on
God, thus letting our heart guide our efforts and
interactions with people, the more we'll feel serene on a daily, even hourly basis.

We now know that God is always with us
offering protection, guidance, and security. This
makes it possible to handle even the most difficult situations where logic failed to work before.
We're never given more than we can handle, but
we must go within ourselves for quiet direction
on how to proceed through the stormy elements.

---

*I will trust my heart in all matters today. Certain and
loving guidance lives there.*

*We all carry our own deep wound, which
is the wound of our loneliness.*
— *Jean Vanier*

How often we suffer needlessly, having made
a decision to be lonely. Yes, a decision. Loneliness
doesn't just happen. We are free to join with others. We know that. Our friends, like us, need
friends. It is not an imposition to get in touch and
say, "Hi, I need to talk," or, "How about a cup of
coffee?" We welcome these overtures from our
friends, as they welcome ours.

Loneliness comes from a feeling of separation,
the idea that we are different. One of the most
remarkable gifts of our program is coming to see
that we are all God's children. God gave us each
other, and we are far more alike than different.
We are never alone except by choice. We can join
our Higher Power at any instant and be comforted. And we can join our friends in the knowledge that they need us as we need them.

*The wound of loneliness is self-inflicted, and I am
healed by remembering God, or joining with others.*

Love is the only sane and satisfactory
answer to the problem of human
existence.
— *Erich Fromm*

How often we unnecessarily complicate our life. We create conflicts with our friends and with people we don't even know, draining ourselves physically, emotionally, and spiritually. We worry about who's right, who's in charge, and we become brittle. We forget God.

Why do we expend our precious energy in this way when showing patience and love is so much easier? Love fills us with energy. Love softens us as it heals our hidden wounds. Love enlightens us as to God's role in our life. And those who receive our love are softened and healed and enlightened as well.

The life we've been given by God is meant for enjoyment. But we can be certain of this enjoyment only when we put our energy into actions that replenish our soul. Love guarantees replenishment by guaranteeing our connection to God, from whom our sanity and peace come.

I will listen to God's will today and, instead of conflict, offer love at every opportunity.

There are two kinds of people: those who say to God, "Thy will be done," and those to whom God says, "All right, then, have it your way."

— *C. S. Lewis*

The will of God isn't forced on us. There are times, though, when we wish it was. Often, those are the times we have taken our free will and run too far with it. God always gives us as much rope as we wish, and we make the choice to trip ourselves, hang ourselves, or maybe just tie ourselves in knots.

When we sincerely say, "Thy will be done," and let go, amazing things happen. Often problems vanish, animosities soften into friendliness, fear is replaced by confidence, and hatred turns to love. All it takes is making a decision. Turning our will and our life over to something or someone else is beyond the ability of most of us. God settles for willingness, and gladly does the rest for us.

Today, I'll follow God's path.

Anger dwells only in the bosom of fools.
— *Albert Einstein*

Anger can be a healthy emotion, provided we don't wallow in it or attack other people. When we express anger honestly and without reservation, we can prevent walls of resentment from building up and blocking us off from the intimacy that we strive for in our relationships.

When we allow anger to fester in our heart, we surrender our peace of mind and lose our sense of purpose and self-worth. When we harbor anger rather than openly and respectfully expressing it, we no longer hear our inner spirit. Thus we are cut off from our innate wisdom to guide us in our actions.

We're often drawn to people who express their feelings honestly. This style of communicating serves as an invitation to build a relationship with them based on trust. From this trust we learn to open ourselves to God's love for us *as we are.*

Today I will feel my anger, express it when necessary, and then let it go so that I can deepen my trust of other people and of God.

Ignore previous cookie.
    — Message in fortune cookie

We live in a throwaway age. Light bulbs, washing machines, all kinds of electronic gizmos, automobiles, packaged foods, clothing, economics, political ideals — all, it seems, have built-in obsolescence. Many things wear out just after the warranty expires.

The principles of our program do not wear out. Love, honesty, humility, gratitude — these have withstood the test of time because they are set on a spiritual foundation. The love of God is eternal. When we reflect that kind of love in our relationships, they prosper and last. God's love never needs to be traded in for next year's model, and the warranty never runs out.

I am grateful for our enduring principles.

Where love rules, there is no will to
power; and where power predominates,
there love is lacking.

— *Carl Jung*

As we work our program we learn about powerlessness. We learn that we are powerless over
much of what shapes our life except our own
attitudes and behavior. When we forget this and
try to control other people's behavior or feelings,
we destroy our serenity and theirs. When we dig
in our heels, certain that our ideas are best, each
moment is filled with tension, and whatever joy
and peace there might have been is dissipated.

Working our program has also taught us about
acceptance and flexibility. When we bend a little
and accept ourselves and others for who we are
in the moment, joy and peace flourish. We become
enriched and free to receive what God has to give
us through each situation or relationship.

All we need to know about living a life of
peace and joy will be shown us.

I will relax and accept God's lesson about living peace-
fully and joyfully today.

*An intellectual is a person whose mind
watches itself.*

— *Albert Camus*

Obsessing can be a deadly habit. If we're
thinking too much, we can't enjoy what's going
on around us. How can we appreciate the beauty
of this world and the people who inhabit it unless
we stop watching ourselves so closely?

We do, of course, need to be aware of our
shortcomings. But once we've asked God to remove them, we don't need to constantly spy on
ourselves mentally to see if we're about to make a
blunder. Self-absorption is the enemy of serenity.
Peace of mind comes from trusting God and
turning our attention to others — not to their
faults, but to their assets, and then showing God
and them our appreciation.

*Today I will look outward to God and others, and
experience moments of peace.*

The one important thing I have learned over the years is the difference between taking one's work seriously and taking one's self seriously. The first is imperative and the second is disastrous.
— *Margot Fonteyn*

We know that it's not really the end of the world when we make a major blunder, but we often act as though it is. We shudder with shame, certain that our co-workers and friends will now completely revise their opinions of us. Our grandiosity cultivates this kind of shame. We forget that we're human and, being human, we make mistakes. We create standards of perfection impossible to meet, and doom ourselves to feel like failures.

Fortunately, this doesn't have to be a permanent condition. We can come to trust that God's love is not contingent on our meeting some ideal standard of behavior. God loves us *because* we're human (and therefore fallible), not in spite of it.

If God wants anything for us, it is that we find joy in life. We find this best with joyful people.

I will seek out and experience joy today.

*For my part I would rather smoke one
cigar than hear two sermons.*
— *Robert G. Ingersoll*

Newcomers to our program need the understanding of people like us who have had the same
experiences, have faced the same humiliation, the
same despair. They probably heard preaching
most of their lives and didn't come into this program to hear more. They need to hear from us
how we found a better way of life.

In this program we don't preach. Instead, we
offer understanding and love. God's unconditional love came to us through men and women
who had been through the same ordeals we had.
And as we grow and recover, we learn that if we
want to keep this love, we have to pass it on.

---

*I will resist the impulse to preach to newcomers. In-
stead, I will give them understanding and love.*

Practice being excited.

— Bill Foster

The happiness, love, and serenity we long for can become a reality when we're willing to Act as If. This may sound like magic, but it isn't. Many of us have been timid, depressed, or angry for so long, and these feelings have become so familiar, that we've gotten stuck. Yet we can free ourselves, and instead get stuck in the feelings that exhilarate us.

We may be doubtful when we hear people say things like, "We're as happy as we make up our mind to be." But in many ways we are. No one else has the power to decide for us how we feel and who we are. As we become aware of the choices we have for new behaviors, we're responsible for choosing the actions that encourage positive feelings over the negative ones.

We can become a person who is ready with laughter, who sees joy more than sadness, who feels gratitude more than disappointment. We can enjoy life just as fully as anyone we know. God has given each of us a measure of wonder.

Today I will find as much joy as I can in every event.

*Art, like morality, consists of drawing the
line somewhere.*

— *G. K. Chesterton*

We don't come into this program with the same
ideas on what constitutes moral or immoral con-
duct. There will always be differences between
us. But formulating moral values was never one
of the functions of our program. Working the
Twelve Steps to the best of our ability determines
our behavior.

Sooner or later, all of us realize that we have to
draw our own moral lines somewhere. A good
way to develop our moral values is to observe
some program old-timers we admire. It seldom
hurts to emulate winners. And we can hold on to
our values by working the Eleventh Step, maintaining a conscious contact with God.

*Today I will draw the line at anything that blocks me
from my Higher Power.*

I look back on my life like a good day's work,
it was done and I am satisfied with it.
— *Grandma Moses*

We have matured when we believe our best is good enough. With the help of our program and our Higher Power, we no longer insist on perfection; we know progress is enough to expect. Putting focused effort into our job, a home project, or a relationship is our only assignment today. When we give our honest effort, God will take care of the outcome.

Many of us look at our past with disgust. Perhaps we failed in some way or lost something that was important to us. Whatever has happened, our best attitude now is acceptance, trusting that we did the best we could at that time.

We are growing and changing; our understanding of how the program works has deepened. Each moment we try to find our purpose promises us many moments of fulfillment. Our Higher Power is directing us toward the right path.

I will look for God's instructions today. I can always be sure of progress when I listen.

*"I can forgive but I cannot forget" is only
another way of saying "I cannot forgive."*
— Henry Ward Beecher

Forgiveness has no degrees; we either do or
we don't. To say we can't forget simply means
we are still holding a grudge, a big fat resentment. And that, for us, is deadly. When we came
into this program, our new friends held nothing
against us. Their forgiveness was complete; for
them it was as if the bad things we did never
happened.

So it is with God's forgiveness of us. God
doesn't care what we did. God loves us now. God
always takes us as we are. Should we do less for
those who have harmed us? Should we do less
for ourselves? Remember, the faults we see in
others are our own, and the resentments we hold
against others are the same we hold against ourselves. Forgiveness frees others as it frees us.

***

Today I will forgive and forget so I can be free.

*A clay pot sitting in the sun will always
be a clay pot. It has to go through the
white heat of the furnace to become
porcelain.*
— *Mildred W. Struven*

Our pain teaches us compassion for others.
We're strengthened through every painful experience we survive. Anyone who has lost a loved
one knows that the initial devastation lessens with
time. And sharing the hope for survival with a
friend now going through a loss strengthens us
again, while it strengthens him or her.

Struggles are natural to life. If we experience
them with the belief that God is always with us,
our struggles will give us perspective, character,
and a clearer vision of our purpose. But most of
all, we will again have hope for the future. Each
hurdle we master lessens the fear for tomorrow.

I can let God lead me through the rough terrain today.

Wise sayings often fall on barren ground,
but a kind word is never thrown away.
— *Arthur Helps*

As we recover, we improve in many ways, but God doesn't necessarily make us flawless communicators. Nor does God suddenly give us greater intelligence. Reliance on God does, however, enable us to live up to our potential.

God offers everyone a gift that overshadows all others — the capacity to give and receive love. And when we have this gift, there is nothing more we truly need. We may not be able to bring an audience to the edge of their seats, or offer our friends gems of wisdom, but we can recognize when someone is hurting and offer a kind word.

Today I will be kind to others.

*No passion so effectively robs the mind of
all its powers of acting and reasoning as
fear.*
— *Edmund Burke*

We know, intellectually at least, that if we turn
our life and our will over to God, we have nothing
to fear. Though we may do Step Three on a daily
basis, some situations still surprise or baffle us.

Some days we may need to remind ourselves
moment by moment that God is in charge. And
that's okay. Just because our ego forgets about
God and tries to fix problems doesn't mean we're
failures. It only means it's time to pause, remind
ourselves of who is in charge, and quiet our mind.
God can then reach us with the right message
about what to do next.

Let's be assured that we will become less fearful in the months and years ahead. In fact, we are
already more relaxed, confident, and serene than
we were before finding our recovery program.
We now trust the promise that ". . . God is doing
for us what we could not do for ourselves."

*When fearful today, I will calm down and listen for
God's message.*

*Growth begins when we start to accept
our own weakness.*

— *Jean Vanier*

We thought we were self-sufficient, that we needed no help to run our life, but this got us into trouble. We discovered that willpower was useless in extricating ourselves from our addictions. We realized we weren't quite as strong and independent as we had imagined. It was in surrendering to that truth and asking for help that we began to recover.

Many of us would just as soon leave it at that. *Addiction is one thing, daily living another,* we think. But in thinking that, we limit our growth. We need help in all areas of living. And when we admit our weakness, we get help. Saying to God, "I don't know what to do," is the quickest way to learn.

---

*Today I am powerless over people, places, and things.
My growth depends on remembering that.*

Until you know that life is interesting —
and find it so — you haven't found your
soul.

— Geoffey Fisher

Abe Lincoln is supposed to have said, "We're just as happy as we make up our minds to be" — which is another way of saying, "We get out of life just what we put in." Rather than watching events pass us by, we can risk leaping into the action of the moment and being participants.

As participants, we discover our inner goals and talents. We begin communicating with others, taking risks, and allowing ourselves to be vulnerable. The road isn't always smooth but, by opening ourselves to both the hardships and triumphs that come with taking responsibility for our life, we learn our own depths and the depths of others. As participants, the richness of life's opportunities gradually becomes apparent as our knowledge of ourselves and others grows. We discover the fullness of our soul.

I will move from the sidelines today and participate in life so that I may explore the depths of my soul and grow.

Logic never attracts men to the point of carrying them away.
— *Alexis Carrell*

In all the world's great literature, there have been countless odes to love but few if any to logic. Love obviously excites more interest and passion. Then why do we base so many of our actions on logic alone? Is it that we don't think we'll be respected if we can't show how logical our reasoning is?

The world's vast store of spiritual literature is replete with appeals to love; God wants us to be carried away with it. Over and over again we are urged to love one another as we love ourselves. Our mind, a wondrous instrument indeed, is strictly utilitarian. Love is the vital component of our being.

Today I will respect my mind, but also heed my heart.

*Love cures people, the ones who receive
love and the ones that give it, too.*
— *Karl A. Menninger*

We are healing our physical and spiritual selves
every time we greet another human being with
kind and gentle attention. And our loving expression will heal and soothe the spirit of our
friend as well.

When we are ill, we remember how much we
are powerless over; but we are not powerless
over how we act or think or feel. And all three
contribute powerfully to our personal well-being
— physically, mentally, and spiritually.

Our behavior — how we direct our thoughts
and feelings — has a powerful impact on the
people in our life as well. We complicate our life
by mean-spiritedness, making ourselves and
others sick and sad. Not one of us is helped —
ever — by cruel expressions, whether openly
shared or only quietly harbored. No expression
misses its mark.

Our health is certain to be hindered by hate
and, just as certainly, it is helped by the smallest
measure of love.

---

*God's hope for me is true health and happiness as I
seek to express God's love today.*

*With them I gladly shared my all and
learned the great truth that where God
guides, He provides.*
— *Frank N. D. Buchman*

Do we believe that God will provide if we let
go? Are we willing to turn everything in our care
over to the care of God?

It's a difficult test of our faith to turn everything
over to God. It's not too hard to say, "Okay, God,
here's my will." We may not even be sure what
that means. But what about giving up our whole
life? We know what "everything" means. It means
giving to God our way of making a living, of
taking care of our families. It means entrusting to
God our health, our friends, our habits, even our
next meal.

We may never be called upon to give up our
possessions, to change our occupation, to go to a
strange place. But unless we listen and become
willing to give God everything, we will never feel
the full comfort of God's care.

*Today it's my decision to give God everything, and to
let God provide.*

*To have reason to get up in the morning,
it is necessary to possess a guiding
principle, a belief of some kind.*
— *Judith Guest*

How much easier it is to face the conflicts in our job and relationships when we remember that we're here, now, for a purpose—by design. We don't need to understand the purpose or know the outcome of a situation that's causing us anxiety. To feel relief from our worries, we need only remember that outcomes belong with life's ultimate designer—God. We are only responsible for our efforts.

Many of us have to consciously remind ourselves that there is a designer in charge and a design to how life unfolds. We can grasp this with our mind, but we also need to know in our heart that we are a part of this unfolding. Trust in this can be developed through practicing prayer and meditation. In time, as we understand God's will for us more deeply, we'll face each new day certain that it has been carefully designed and that we have a special part to play in it.

I will find my purpose and direction today by asking for God's will for me.

Compassion is the basis of all morality.
— *Arthur Schopenhauer*

We can have cash-register honesty and still be immoral. We can be faithful to our partners, diligent in our work, scrupulous in paying our debts, careful not to gossip, and determined not to steal from anyone — yet God will take little notice if we are not loving. The basis of our recovery program is compassion and love for one another.

Our understanding of each other's feelings and our desire to help is the foundation of our recovery. We are never as close to God as in our compassionate moments. That's when we know the true meaning of morality. That's when we know God.

I remember the compassion that brought me to recovery. May my actions today be a reflection of that love.

Conscience is the perfect interpreter of life.
— *Karl Barth*

Our conscience swiftly informs us when we've made a rash judgment or responded too harshly to someone. We can trust this as a reminder from God that we're veering off our spiritual path.

How lucky we are that within all of us there's a source of spiritual guidance where we can turn for direction in our life, and it is always available to us. Of course, we may refuse to listen, particularly when we're in an ego struggle with someone. We sometimes choose to obsessively focus our mind on our efforts to control another person, and this effectively prevents us from receiving the guidance offered by our Higher Power. If we opened ourselves to God's guidance, our behavior could immediately and dramatically change.

It's comforting to know that we always have direction available to take the right action, respond in the best way, and make the right choices. Our loving Guide awaits within to help us every step of our way.

If I get quiet for just a moment before speaking or acting, I'll not be sorry today.

*God forces no one, for love cannot
compel, and God's service, therefore, is a
thing of perfect freedom.*

— *Hans Denk*

Although God is all-powerful, we are not forced to love God. Love attracts; it doesn't compel or promote, just as our Twelve Step program, based on love, attracts rather than promotes. The Steps are suggested, never required. We are free to pick and choose; we can take from our program what we find useful and discard the rest.

Most of the veterans of our program, however, take it all because the program works best in its entirety. Rather than discarding parts of the program, we discard those things that block us from God's love. It is our own behavior that can keep us from enjoying spiritual gifts. We are free to be just as close to — or as far from — God as we wish.

Today I will exercise my freedom to enjoy God's love, and all the comfort, inspiration, and help that comes with it.

Hunting God is a great adventure.
— Marie DeFloris

Eventually, most of us discover it's not very difficult to find God somewhere in our life. We may find God in the simple beauty of a flower when we're out for a walk in the woods. Or we may experience God working through the women and men who share our journey. In time, many of us come to believe that God is everywhere, always, and never more than a thought or a breath away.

When we have achieved full acceptance that wherever else God is manifest, God is within *us* too, we'll walk easier through our dark and troubling times. But even when we know that God is with us every moment, we may forget. Then, just pausing and praying for help will relieve our anxiety, and God's presence will be felt.

We may still fear the outcome of a situation because we're not certain God wants the same things for us that we want. But by recalling our past, when God's direction has brought us where we need to be, we can rest our mind and turn our life over again.

I'll remember that I don't have to look very far for God today.

Show me what a man envies the least in others and I will show you what he has got the most of himself.

— Josh Billings

It's a little disconcerting to discover that the faults we deplore in others are exactly the ones we're dealing with too. A person who berates a partner, friend, or co-worker for being too critical is demonstrating the same flaw. Why can't we see our own character flaws, so apparent to others?

Maybe it's because we're dealing with a spiritual principle. Our brothers and sisters are our mirrors. God made us essentially alike. Each of us is as deserving of criticism as anyone, and as worthy of love. When we condemn someone, we condemn ourselves. By loving others, we are loved.

Today I will see others as I want to be seen, and treat them as I want to be treated.

*I would rather live in a world where my
life is surrounded by mystery than live in
a world so small that my mind could
comprehend it.*
— *Henry Emerson Fosdick*

In past years, when we thought of our future,
most of us could never have imagined our life as
it is now. With our mind clouded by our addictions, our dreams were either too small or too
grandiose and unrealistic.

Though we are now mostly free from obsessive thinking, we may still dream too small and
think of a future limited by our specific require-
ments: "I must have this promotion." "My life is
meaningful only if this relationship succeeds."

We can learn to open ourselves to and savor
the mystery of how our life is unfolding. God's
plan that brought us safely here includes the
possibility of an even more fulfilling life. We don't
need to know what we'll be doing five years or
even three days from now. We're in God's loving
care now, as in the past, and we can trust we'll be
just where we need to be in the future.

---

*I can quietly go about my life today trusting that God
is present and that tomorrow will be taken care of too.*

INDEX